QUIET TALKS ON JOHN'S GOSPEL
BY
S. D. Gordon

QUIET TALKS ON JOHN'S GOSPEL

Published by Scriptura Press

New York City, NY

First published circa 1936

Copyright © Scriptura Press, 2015

All rights reserved

Except in the United States of America, this book is sold subject to the condition that it shall not, by way of trade or otherwise, be lent, re-sold, hired out, or otherwise circulated without the publisher's prior consent in any form of binding or cover other than that in which it is published and without a similar condition including this condition being imposed on the subsequent purchaser.

ABOUT SCRIPTURA PRESS

Scriptura Press is a Christian company that makes Christian works available and affordable to all. We are a non-denominational publishing group that shares the teachings of the Scripture, whether in the form of sermons or histories of the Church.

Preface

Everything depends on getting Jesus placed. That lies at the root of all—living, serving, preaching, teaching. John had Jesus placed. He had Him up in His own place. This settles everything else. Then one gets himself placed, too, up on a level where the air is clear and bracing, the sun warm, and the outlook both steadying and stimulating. Get the centre fixed and things quickly adjust themselves about it to your eyes.

It will be seen very quickly that this little book makes no pretension to being a commentary on, or an exposition of, John's Gospel. That is left to the scholarly folk who eat their meals in the sacred classical languages of the past. It is simply a homely attempt to let out a little of what has been sifting in these years past of this wondrous miniature Bible from John's pen.

The proportions of this homely little messenger of paper and type may seem a little odd at first. The longest chapter is devoted to only the opening eighteen verses of John, the prologue. While the whole of the first twelve chapters of John, excepting that prologue, is brought into one smaller chapter. It wasn't planned so, though I felt it coming as the wondrous mood of this book came down over me. I think it mast be the effect of the atmosphere of John's book.

Sometimes John packs so much in so little space, and again he goes so particularly into the details of some one incident. The prologue is a miniature Bible. The whole Bible story is there in its cream. And on the other hand John spends five chapters (xiii.-xvii.), almost a fifth of the whole, on a single evening. He devotes seven chapters (xiii.-xix.), almost a third of all, on the events of twenty-four hours. John is controlled not by mere proportion of space or quantity, but by the finer proportions of thought and quality.

It has been difficult to hold these homely talks down to the limit of space they take here. So many veins of gold in this mine, showing clearly large nuggets of pure ore, lie just at hand untouched in this little mining venture. But it seemed clearly best to get the one clear grasp of the whole. That helps so much. But there'll be strong temptation to get one's pick and spade and go at this gold mine again.

But now these things are written that we common folk may understand a bit better, and in a warm way, that Jesus was God on a wooing errand to the earth; and that we may join the blest company of the won ones, and become co-wooers with God of the others.

I. John's Story

II. The Wooing Lover

Who it was that came.

III. The Lover Wooing

A group of pictures illustrating how the wooing was done and how   the Lover was received.

IV. Closer Wooing

An evening with opening hearts: the story of a supper and a walk in   the moonlight and the shadows.

V. The Greatest Wooing

A night and a day with hardening hearts: the story of tender   passion and of a terrible

tragedy.
  VI. An Appointed Tryst Unexpectedly Kept
  A day of startling joyous surprises.
  VII. Another Tryst
  A story of fishing, of guests at breakfast, and of a walk and talk   by the edge of blue Galilee.

I

John's Story

—Francis Thompson, in "The Hound of Heaven."

"These are written that ye may believe that Jesus is the Christ, the Son of God; and that believing ye may have life in his name."—John xx. 31.

I

John's Story
The Heart-strings of God.

There's a tense tugging at the heart of God. The heart-strings of God are tight, as tight as tight can be. For there's a tender heart that's easily tugged at one end, and an insistent tugging at the other. The tugging never ceases. The strings never slack. They give no signs of easing or getting loose.

It's the tug of man's sore need at the down-end, the man-end, of the strings. And it's the sore tug of grief over the way things are going on down here with men, at the other end, the up-end, the heart-end, of the strings. It's the tense pull-up of a love that grows stronger with the growth of man's misunderstanding.

But the heart-strings never snap. The heart itself breaks under the tension of love and grief, grieved and grieving love. But the strings only strengthen and tighten under the strain of use.

Those heart-strings are a bit of the heart they're tied to, an inner bit, aye the innermost bit, the inner heart of the heart. They are the bit pulled, and pulled more, and pulled harder, till the strings grew. Man was born in the warm heart of God. Was there ever such a womb! Was there ever such another borning, homing place!

It was man's going away that stretched the heart out till the strings grew. The tragedy of sin revealed the toughness and tenderness of love. For that heart never let go of the man whom it borned. Man tried to pull away, poor thing. In his foolish misunderstanding and heady wilfulness he tried to cut loose. If he had known God better he would never have tried that. He'd never have started away; and he'd never have tried to get away.

For love never faileth. A heart—the real thing of a heart, that is, God's heart—never lets go. It breaks; but let go? not once: never yet. The breaking only loosens the red that glues fast with a tighter hold than ever. The fibre of the heart—God's heart—is made of too strong stuff to loosen or wear out or snap. Love never faileth. It can't; because it's love.

Now all this explains Jesus. It was man's pull on these heart-strings that brought Him down. The pull was so strong and steady. It grew tenser and more insistent. And straight down He came by the shortest way, the way of those same heart-strings. For the heart-strings of God are the shortest distance between two given points, the point of God's giving, going love, and the point of man's sore need, given a sharper-pointed end by its very soreness.

It is a sort of blind pull, this pull of man on the heart of God; a confused, unconscious, half-conscious, dust-blinded, slippery-road sort of pulling, but one whose tight grip never slacks. Man needs God, but does not know it. He knows he needs _some_thing. He feels that keenly. But he does not know that it's God whom he needs, with a very few rare exceptions. It doesn't seem to have entered his head that he'll never get out of his tight corner till God gets him out.

Down the street of life he goes, eyes blinded by the thick dust, ears deafened by the cries of the crowd, by the noise of the street without, and the noise of passions and fevered ambitions within, heart a-wearied by the confusion of it all, groping, stumbling, jostled and jostling, hitting this way and that, with the fever high in his blood, and his feet aching and bleeding; sometimes the polish of culture on the surface; _some_times rags and dirt; but underneath the same thing.

Yet under all there's a vague but very real feeling of that unceasing pull upward upon His heart-strings. But though blind and vague and confused that tugging is never the less tense, but ever more, and then yet more.

Jesus was God answering the tug of man's need on His heart-strings. And so naturally there was an answering feel in man's heart. Man felt the answer a-coming. There was a great stir in the spirit-currents of earth when Jesus came. A thrill of expectancy ran through the world, Roman, Greek, Barbarian, far and wide, as Jesus drew near. The book-makers of that time all speak of it. It was the vibration of those same heart-strings connecting man and God.

The move at God's end was felt at man's. The coming down along the highway of the strings thrilled and stirred and awed the hearts into which those strings led, and where they were so tightly knotted. The earth-currents spread the news. Man heard; he felt; he knew: vaguely, blindly, wearily, yet very really he heard and felt and recognized that help, a Friend, some One, was nearing.

And then when Jesus walked among men how He did pull upon their hearts! So quietly He went about. So sympathetically He looked and listened. So warm was the human touch of His hand. So strong was the lift of His arm to ease their load. So potent was the spell of His unfailing power to give relief. How He did pull! And how men did answer to that pull! Unresistingly, eagerly, as weary child in mother's arms at close of day, they came crowding to Him.

The Fourfold Message.

It is fascinating to find one book in this old Book of God given up wholly to telling of this, John's Gospel. Of course the whole of the Book is really given up to it, when one gets the whole simple view of it at one glance. But so many of us don't get that whole simple glance.

So to make it easier for us simple common folk, and to make sure of our getting it, there is one little book, hardly big enough to call a book, just a few pages devoted wholly to letting us see this one thing. You can see the whole of the sun in a single drop of water. You can see the whole of the Book of God in this one little book that John wrote.

John's Gospel is like the small tracing of the artist's pen on the lower corner of an etching, the remarque, put there as a signature, the artist's personal mark that the picture is genuine, the real thing. The whole consummate skill of the artist is revealed at a glance in the simple outline-tracing on the margin. The whole of the God-story in the larger picture of the whole Book is given in few simple clear lines in this exquisite little thing commonly called John's Gospel.

It is striking to make the discovery that John's little book has a distinctive message as a book. It is full of messages, of course. But I mean that there is a distinct story told by the book as a whole, by the very way it is put together. It is told by the very sort of language used, the words chosen as the leading words of the book. It is told by the picture that clearly fills John's eye as he writes, and by the very spirit that floods the pages as a soft light, and that breaks out of them as the subtle fragrance of locust blossoms in the spring.

The fragrance of flowers cannot be analyzed: it must be smelled and felt. That's the only way you'll ever know it. The fine scholarly analyses of John are helpful. But there's the subtler something that cannot be diagramed or analyzed or synthesized. It eludes the razor-edged knife, and the keenly critical survey. It is recognized only by one's spirit, and then only when the spirit is warm, and in tune with John's.

Of course each of the Gospel stories has a message of its own, quite apart from the group of facts common to them all. And these four messages together give us the fuller distinctive message of these four little books. And a very winsome message it is, too, that takes hold of one's heart, and takes a warm strong hold at that.

Matthew tells us that Jesus is a King. For a great purpose He chose to live as a peasant, as one of the common folks. But He was of the blood royal. He has the long unbroken kingly lineage. He showed kingly power in His actions, kingly wisdom in His teachings, and the fine kingly spirit in His gracious kindliness of touch. He was gladly accepted and served as King by those who understood Him best. He was acknowledged as King by the Roman Governor; and He died as a King, and as a King was laid in a newly hewn tomb.

Mark adds a fine touch to this picture, a warm touch with colour in it,—this King of ours is a serving King. This comes not only with a warm feel, but it comes as a distinct surprise. Men's kings are served kings. There have been kings, and are, who rendered their people a fine high service, and do. But the overpowering impression given the common crowd watching on the street is that kings are superior beings, to be waited upon, humbly bowed to, and implicitly obeyed. They are to be served.

Bat Mark's picture shows us a King whose passion is to serve. The service which He draws out of His followers is drawn out by His warm serving spirit towards us. The words on the royal coat-of-arms are, "Not to be ministered unto, but to minister." And in the first meaning of the words He Himself used that means "not to be served but to serve." In Mark the air is tense with rapid action. The quick executive movement of a capable servant is felt in the terse words short sentences and swift action of the story.

There's yet warmer colouring in Luke's picture. This serving King is nearest of kin to us! He is not only of the blood royal, but of the blood human. He is bone of our bone, blood of our blood, and life of our common life. He came to us through a rare union of God's power with human consent and human function, never known before nor repeated since. This is the bit that Luke adds to the composite message of these four little God-story books.

Here Jesus has a tenderness of human sympathy with us men, for He and we are brothers. There's an outlook as broad as the race. No national boundaries limit its reach. No sectional prejudices warp or shut Him off from sympathetic touch with any. He shares our common life. He knows our human temptations, and knows them with a reality that is painful, and with an intensity that wets His brow and shuts His jaw hard.

This king who serves is a man. He can be a king of men for He is a man. He has the first qualification. I might use an old-fashioned word in the first old-time meaning,—He is a fellow, one who shares the bed and bread of our common experience. And so He is kin to us, both in lineage and in experience, in blood and in spirit.

And John's share in this partnership message adds a simple bold touch of colouring that makes the picture a masterpiece, the masterpiece. This King who serves, and is nearest of kin to us, is also nearest of kin to God. He is not only of the blood royal, and the blood human, but of the blood divine. He was with God before calendars came into use. He was the God of that creative Genesis week. He came on an errand down to the earth, and when the errand was done, and well done, He went back home, bearing on His person the marks of His fidelity to the Father's errand. This is John's bit of rich high colouring.

And so we are nearest of kin to God through Jesus. Kinship is always a matter of blood. There is a double kinship, through the blood of inheritance, and the blood of sacrifice. Our inherited kinship of blood has been lost. But His blood of sacrifice has made a new kinship. We had broken the entail of our inheritance clean beyond mending. We were outcasts by our own act. But He cast in. His lot with us, and so drew us back and up and in. He made a new entail through His blood. And that new entail is as unbreakable as the old broken one is unmendable. And so we come into the family of a King. And we are kingliest in character when we are Christliest in spirit and action. We are most like the King when we are helping others.

Our true motto, in our relation to our fellows, is: "I am among you as he that serveth." Towel and basin, bended knee and comforted pilgrim-feet and refreshed spirit,—this is our family crest. We're kin to all the race through Jesus. Black skin and white, yellow and brown; round heads and long, slanting eyes and oval, in slum alley and palatial home, below the equator and above it,—all are our kinsmen.

We are reaching highest when we are stooping lowest to help some one up. We're nearest like God in character when we're getting nearest in touch to those needing help. We are kingliest and Godliest and Christliest when we're controlled by men's needs, but always under the higher control of the Holy Spirit.

This is the composite message of the four Gospels; and this is its practical human outworking. God on a Wooing Errand.

But it's the other John message we are especially after just now. There's another message of John's book quite distinct from this, though naturally allied with it. And this other is the crowding message of his book. Its thought crowds in upon you till every other is crowded into second place. And as it gets hold of you it crowds your mind and heart and life till every other is either crowded out, or crowded to a lower place; out, if it jars; lower place, if it agrees, for every agreeing bit yields to the lead of this tremendous message.

But one must get hold of John before John's message gets hold of him. John was swayed by a passion. It was a fiery passion flaming through all his life. It burned through him as the fierce forest fire burns through the underbrush. Every base thing was eaten up by its flame. Every less worthy thing came under its heat. It melted and mellowed and moulded his whole being.

It was the Jesus-passion. It was kindled that memorable afternoon early in his life down in the Jordan bottoms.[1] John's namesake, the Herald, applied the kindling match. From then on the flames never flickered nor burned low. They increased steadily, and they increased in purity, until his whole life was under their holy heat.

John didn't always understand his Master. Sometimes he misunderstood. But he never failed in his trust of Him, nor in his fidelity to Him. Of the chosen inner circle John was the one who remained true through the sorest test, that betrayal-night test. Judas betrayed; Peter denied; the nine fled in terror down the road to save their cowardly lives; John went in "with Jesus." That fiery nature of his, that early won for him the stormy name "son of thunder," came completely under the sway of this holier tenderer stronger flame, and burned itself out in a passion of love for Jesus.

The Jesus-passion swayed John completely. This explains the man, and his career. It explains this little book of his ripe old age. And only this can. One must read the book through John's own heart, then he begins to understand it. This Jesus-passioned man is the key to the book, the human key.

And the distinctive message of the book is simply this: Jesus was God on a wooing errand to the earth. That simple sentence covers fully all that is found in John's twenty-one chapters. Every line in these fourteen or fifteen pages can be traced back into that brief statement.

Indeed this becomes an outline of the book. See: in the opening paragraphs the wooing Lover is coming down to earth.[2] In the first twelve chapters the Lover is pleading winsomely and earnestly for acceptance.[3] Then He is seen in closest touch with the inner group of those who have accepted, opening His heart yet more, wooing still closer.[4] Then comes the last tragic pleading, pleading in intensest action, with those who persist in rejecting.[5] And then the last close heart-touches with the inner circle.[6]

The Water-Mark of John's Gospel.

The very words John so thoughtfully chooses as his leading words bear the distinct impress of this, like the sharply indented stamp of the mint on the new coin. Two such words stand out above all others, "believe" and "witness." The first actually occurs oftenest, sounding out like the dominant chord of music running throughout a symphony. The second is like the chief warp-thread into which the fabric is being woven.

The two words are really twins, born at the same time, of the same mother. They grow up together and work in perfect accord. The witnessing is that men may understand and believe. It's the servant leading up to the belief that shall become the mastering thing. The belief is servant, too, in turn, leading up to the witnessing that becomes the mastering passion in those who believe.

These words are worth digging into for the fine gold that lies hidden within waiting the miner's pick. The word "believe" is a nugget of pure gold, whether you take our English word or John's word lying underneath. The underneath word, that John uses in his own mother tongue, runs a sliding scale of meaning.

It's a ladder rising from bottom round to topmost. It means to be persuaded that a thing is true; then to place confidence in it, to trust. And trust always contains the idea of risk. The heart-meaning always is that you risk something very precious to you, risk it to the point of heart-breaking disaster if your trust proves wrong.

Our English word is of very close kin. It runs the same sort of sliding scale, from something valuable and precious in itself, on to something that satisfies you regarding the matter in hand. You are not only satisfied but pleased, content. And so there is the same trusting and risking, the same leaning your whole weight upon the thing. Deep down at its root, believe is a close kinsman to love. They both spring out of the same warm creative womb.

When we dig a bit into that word believe in the usage of common life it means three distinct things, each leading straight into the other,—knowledge, belief, trust. That is, facts, facts accepted, facts trusted in regard to something that takes hold of your life. You hear something. You believe it's true. But there must be the third thing, risking something valuable. There's no belief in the heart-meaning without this thing of risking. The trust that risks is the life blood of faith. The rest is only the bony skeleton with tendons and sinews and flesh. There's no life without the blood. There's no belief without trust.

And the word witness is the same pure-gold sort of nugget, assaying full weight. John's native word and our own are just the same in meaning. Their meaning is to tell what you know. We shall be running across this word again, and digging a bit deeper into it. But this is the thing that stands out in it. You tell something that you yourself know. There's personal knowledge. There's a telling some one else this thing you know. And yet more, there's the purpose in the telling, that others may know what you know, and get all the good that comes with knowing it.

The witnessing is that others may believe. It is a striking thing in John that the thought of witness is more common than the word. The word occurs several times, and always in a leading way. But the thought of witnessing is the colouring of every page, and the chief colouring.

I said that these two words were twins, born at the same time, of the same mother. That warm-hearted brooding mother is the word wooing. Originally wooing means bending towards, inclining forward or reaching out towards another. And the purpose of the reaching out is to get the other to reach forward towards you. And that purpose puts the warm feel into the reaching out.

All words were pictures first. Here in this word wooing is a picture, by one of the old masters, waiting to be restored, with all the dusty accumulations of the years carefully removed. And here's the picture: a man standing, with the light of the morning shining in His eyes, body bending forward, hands reaching out, with an eagerness, an expectancy in every line of His body, and tender love glowing out of His face, and sounding in the very tones with which the voice is calling.

This picture is really the water-mark on the paper of John's Gospel. Hold up the paper of John's Gospel to the light. The best light for the purpose is found on Mount Calvary. High altitudes have clearer light. You see more distinctly. Now look. Hold still that you may see all the outlines more distinctly. There's the form of a Man standing in pleading attitude, with outstretched hands. His face combines all the fineness of the finest woman's face, with all the strength of the strongest man's, and more, immensely more, all the purity and tenderness and power of God's face. It is God Himself in human form coming a-wooing to earth, and we call His name Jesus. This conception is the very atmosphere of John's Gospel.

Jesus is the witness of the Father to men. He knew the Father. He knew

Him by closest intimacy. He lived with Him. He came down to tell what He knew. He wanted others to know too. He wanted them to know even as He knew. Telling is the whole of Jesus; telling men of the Father.

His mere presence, His character, His warm sympathy, His practical helpfulness, His words, His actions, most of all His dying and His rising, all these were a telling, a witnessing, a wooing; telling the Father's love, telling the damnableness of our sin by giving His very life blood to get it out of us; so telling us how we might really know the mother-heart of the Father.

Jesus the Dividing Line.

There are several contrasts between the first three Gospels and John's. It is very striking to notice one in particular in this connection. One reading the first three Gospels for the first time is impressed with the fact of Jesus' rejection. This stands out peculiarly and dominantly. It was the great fact, told most terribly in the death of Jesus. It was the thing that stood out sharpest in the generation to which Jesus belonged, the generation for whom these three Gospels were written at the first.

But John wrote his story for an after-generation, a generation that had not known the man Jesus by personal touch and observation. And so it was for all after-generations. And John makes it very clear that Jesus was rejected, and accepted.

He was indeed rejected; that fact stands out as painfully here as in the others. He was rejected by the little inner clique that held the national reins, and held them with fevered tenacity, and drove hard. And the reason for it is made to stand out as plainly as the fact. The envy and jealousy, the intense bitterness and viciousness and devilish obstinacy back of the rejection stand as boldly out to all eyes as to Pilate's.

But the other side stands out sharply too. Jesus was accepted. He was accepted by all classes, by the cultured, and the scholarly, by thoughtful studious leaders and officials of the nation. He was accepted by the great middle classes and by those in lowest scale socially, and by the moral outcasts. Intense Hebrews, Roman officials of high rank, half-breed Samaritans, and men of outside nations group themselves together by their full acceptance of Jesus.

He was listened to, doubted, questioned, discussed, thought over, and then accepted. And He was accepted with a faith and with a love that counted not suffering nor sacrifice for the sake of Him whom they believed and trusted and loved. John makes this clear, rejected and accepted.

Jesus divided the crowds. Down the road He comes, with quiet strength, witnessing to the great simple truth of the Father's pure strong wooing love. And the crowd looks and listens and—divides. Some reject; clearly they are a minority, but entrenched in a position of power that proves quite sufficient for their purpose. Though it took all the power at their command to carry out their purpose.

Others accept. These are the crowds, the majority. Some don't understand. Their motives are selfish or mixed, like some other folks' motives. Some are played upon by the cunning of the leaders and swung away. But there remain the thoughtful ones whose faith goes from weakness to strength; it grows from more to yet more. It mellows from a true simple faith to a deepened, seasoned, sorely-tested, surely-toughened faith that loves, loves clear down to the roots, and endures gladly. This is the simple warp-thread into which John's very simple story of Jesus is woven.

Spelling God.

I want to give you a bunch of keys, as we start into these homely talks in John's Gospel. They are simple keys. Any one can use them. They fit easily and smoothly into every lock, the lock of your life, the lock of any circumstance, any sore problem that may come up to baffle all your efforts. They bring treasures within easy reach. They open up the way into all you need. There is a key to God, a key to the Book of God, and then there are three keys to this little John book.

The key to God is in one little word. It has two spellings, sometimes with four letters, sometimes with five, and both correct spellings. The four-lettered spelling is for all the world. The five-lettered spelling is chiefly used in the western half of the earth, and along certain lines and in certain spots here and there in the eastern half where the word is known.

That first spelling is l-o-v-e. God is love. Love is of God. God is always controlled by a purpose in all His dealings with the race, and with you and me. There is no chance-happening with Him, no caprice, no shadow in His path that tells of His being swerved aside, by anything we do, from a steady purpose.

And that controlling purpose is always a purpose of love. It's a purpose of strong steady pure clinging brooding love. The bother is we don't know what that word love means; none of us. We know words but not the real things they stand for. We don't know the real thing of love because we don't know the real thing of God. If we knew, oh! if we but knew it—Him—how that simple statement would melt us down, and mellow us through, and mould us all over anew!

That's the shorter spelling. It is the universal spelling. That love is being spelled out to all the race by every twinkling star in the upper blue, every shade of green in the lower brown, by every cooling shading night, and every fragrantly dewy morning. Every breath of air and bite of food and draught of water is repeating God's spelling lesson. These are the pages in God's primer. So we all may learn to spell out God. And so we get the right spelling of our own lives.

Then there's the other spelling, the five-lettered, J-e-s-u-s. It's the same thing, only spelled differently; spelled in a yet better way. The spelling grows bigger to us when Jesus comes. When we know Him it takes more to spell out and to tell out God's love. God grows larger to our eyes as He comes walking among us as Jesus. No, He doesn't grow larger. We simply begin to find out how large He is.

This is the closer, more human spelling. The letters are nearer and seem bigger as they come walking down the street where we live, and knock at our own door. They're easier spelled out. We can get hold of them better. Love is a thing, we think. Jesus is a person. It's so different to touch a person. But when we know, we know that both spellings tell the same thing. So far, only about a third of us have heard anything about this second, this closer spelling. Two out of three haven't heard about it yet. But those who really know this spelling are eager for the others to get it, too.

God is always controlled by a great simple purpose in thinking of you and me. And it is an unfailing purpose of strong tender love. This is the first key. Any one may take it and use it. It is unfailing. It will fit every lock. It unlock every problem. It will open up the riches to any life. They're brought within easy reach of any hand by the steady use of this key.

This is the key to God. It unlocks the doors and lets Him freely into our lives. Then we find out how much truer it is than we can understand.

Then there's the key to the Book of God. There are many keys here, of course. Daily time alone with the Book, thoughtful reading, prayer, some simple plan, putting into your life what has been put in its pages,—these are all good keys. But there's a master-key, the master-key. It is simply this: glad surrender of will to the God of the Book. I mean a strong intelligent yielding to His mastery in all of one's plans and life. The highest act of the strongest will is yielding to a higher will when you find it. And you find the higher, the highest, will here.

This is the master-key. Bending the will affects eyes and ears and mind. The hinges of eye and ear are in the will. As the will bends those hinges move of themselves. Eye and ear and mind open. The lower the will bends, the more fully and habitually, the more will eyes and ears open, the keener and more alert will be the mental processes, the more intelligent the understanding. And there comes to be a continual mutual shifting. With better understanding can come stronger more intelligent yielding of will, and so again clearer light.

And it is striking to discover that there's a practical connection between the joints of the knees and the joint of the will. The bending of knees to a sharp right angle affects the will. It is easier to bend it. It bends better and more. And this grows. The habitual bending of the knees helps make habitual and stronger and more intelligent the bending of the will.

This is the master-key to the Book of God. It opens every lock and page. It opens us to the Book, and opens the Book to us. It frees out to us the wondrous Spirit who is in these pages. And so through the opened Book there come to be the direct touch with the God of the Book. We don't come to the Book merely; we come through it to Him who comes through it to us. This is the second key in this bunch.

Three Keys.

Now, I want to give you the three keys to John's Gospel. There's a back-door key, a side-door key, and a front-door key. These keys hang outside the doors, low down, that so any one who wants to can easily reach up, and get them. And if used faithfully and simply they will be found to unlock every page and line and difficult question.

The back-door key hangs right at the back door. It is the very last verse of chapter twenty. That really was the last chapter at first. The thought of the book comes to a close there. The story is complete. Then the Holy Spirit led John to add a little, a second last-chapter, an added touch for good measure. Love is never content. It is always adding more.

Here is the key: "these are written that ye may believe that Jesus is the Christ, the Son of God; and that believing ye may have life through His name." This was John's whole thought in telling the Jesus-story. The practical gripped him wholly and hard. This is the thing that guides his selection of incidents. This purpose shapes the shape of the book. It explains everything told, and just why it is told in just the way it is told.

John lets Jesus walk before our eyes fresh from His Father's presence. The mere fact of His presence, the winsomeness of His personality, the clearness of His teaching, the power of His actions, the uncompromising purity of His character amidst sin-stained crowds and sin-dirtied surroundings, the unflinching rigidity of His ideals, the persuasiveness of His very manner and tone of speech, the patience and gentleness, the rugged granite strength, the mother tenderness, above all the willingness to suffer so terribly,—all this is a plea, a tremendous overpowering plea, all the stronger because presented so simply and briefly. Jesus is a Lover and this is His wooing.

And John's one thought in writing is the same as the one thought in the Lover's heart. John has become simply an echo of Jesus. It is this, that you, whoever you are, wherever, whatever, that you may believe. You look and listen, question, puzzle a bit maybe, but keep on listening and looking, thinking, weighing, till you are clear these things are just so as John tells them. You accept them as trustworthy. Then you accept Him, Jesus, as He comes to you, your wooing Lover, your Lover-God, your Saviour and Lord.

You believe: that is you love. The grammar of the word works itself out inside you thus,—believe, trust, love. The truth comes in through eyes and ears and feeling, into brain and will; through emotion clear down into your heart. You love. You cannot help yourself. You love Him, Jesus, the One so lovable.

John says that you may believe. It is possible. It is the reasonable intelligent thing to do after such a presentation. John makes it easy for us to believe. His telling of the story is so strong and convincing, though so simple and short, that believing is the natural thing. Jesus Himself, as He comes to us through John's eyes and speech, is so believable, so trustworthy, so lovable.

Now we may believe. It's the thing to do after a thoughtful kneeful study of the case as put by John. We may believe clear into and through intellect and emotions and will, right down into the depths of heart and love, clear out into every action of the life.

And John sweeps in the whole crowd of the world in the way he puts it here. Listen: "that you may believe that Jesus is the Christ." That was for the Jew peculiarly in the first instance. The Jew had been taught through generations that there was One coming who was God's chosen One for the Hebrew nation. He was the Anointed One. The Hebrew said Messiah. The Greek said Christ. Both mean the same, the One chosen of God, anointed by Him as the King and Leader of His chosen people, and through them of all the race.

Listen further: "that Jesus is the Son of God." That is for all of us, Jew and foreigner, insider and outsider. This Jesus is in a distinctive sense the Son of God, the only begotten Son. This pure loving pleading wooing suffering dying rising-again Jesus, this is the only begotten Son of the Father. All there is in a Father comes to, and is in, an only begotten son. This is God Himself coming to us in His Son.

Once let this sift into thought and heart, then who would not believe, and trust, and love, and fall on his face in the utter devotion of a voluntary slave before such a God!

And so believing, trusting, loving, touching, His life flows in and fills up and floods out. We have it now. That word eternal, used so often by John with the word life, is not a mere length word. It is not a calendar word. It tells the sort of life, the quality of life, that comes in through the opening door of our believing. This is John's back-door key, but it lets you clear in through the whole house.

Then there is the side-door key. It hangs at the side, a bit towards the back. It is in the Thursday night talk, as we commonly call it, that last heart-talk with the inner group on the betrayal night. It is in chapter sixteen, verse twenty-eight: "I came out from the Father, and am come into the world: again, I leave the world, and go unto the Father."

Run through this Gospel with that fresh in your mind, and it is perfectly fascinating to find how much like a magnet it is, picking out to itself so many bits from the Master's lips that fit exactly into it. Jesus' constant thought was that He used to be with the Father; He came down on an errand to the earth. By and by when the errand was done He would go back home again.

This sentence becomes a simple, exact, comprehensive outline of the entire Gospel. Notice: "I came out from the Father": that is chapter one, verses one to eighteen. There Jesus is seen coming down from His Father's own presence. Then chapter one, verse nineteen through to the close of the twelfth chapter is fully described and covered by the next clause, "and am come into the world." Here He is seen in the world, in the midst of its crowds and contentions and oppositions.

"Again, I leave the world,"—chapters thirteen to nineteen. In chapters thirteen to seventeen He is tenderly leaving the inner circle. In chapters eighteen and nineteen He is going out of the world by the terrible doorway of the cross it had carpentered for Him. How quietly He says the words, though the terrible going is yet to come, and is now so near that He can already feel the shame and the thorns and the nails.

And as quietly He looks beyond and adds, "and go unto the Father." In chapters twenty and twenty-one He lingers a little for the sake of these being left behind, but His face is already turned homeward. They would hold Him in their midst. He quietly tells them that He is going back home to the Father to get things ready for them, as He had said.

He Comes to His Own.

The front-door key hangs right at the very front, outside, low down, where even a child's hand can reach it. It is in chapter one, verses eleven and twelve: "He came unto His own, and they that were His own received Him not. But as many as received Him to them gave He the right to become children of God, even to them who believe on His name." This is the great key, the chief key to this whole house. It flings the front door wide open and you are inside at once, and take in the whole of the house at a glance, one glance, one wonderful glance.

The first twelve chapters tell of Jesus coming to His own, His own nation, humanly, racially, His own chosen people. He is coming steadily and persistently, in spite of rebuffs; coming patiently, tenderly, earnestly; coming ever closer in the ever increasing measure of divine power seen in His actions.

And continually, persistently, He is being rejected and accepted. He is rejected silently and contemptuously, then aggressively and bitterly, viciously and murderously. "His own received Him not." But many received Him, eagerly and warmly and thoughtfully. They received Him with a growing depth of conviction and deepening tenderness of love. And as they come, He is ever receiving them, giving them that touch of new life that marks only the children of God.

In chapters thirteen to seventeen He is receiving into closer fellowship those who have received Him, and at the same time wooing them into yet closer touch. The story of the trial and crucifixion in chapters eighteen and nineteen, puts the most terrific emphasis on the words, "received Him not." They not only keep Him out of His own possessions, but do their worst in putting Him out of life. And the little book closes in its last two chapters with His receivers being received into the sweetest intimacies of tested triumphant love and into the inner secrets of rarest resurrection power.

This is the most heart-breaking of all of John's heart-breaking sentences. John had a hard time writing this Gospel of his. He was not simply writing a book; that might have been fairly easy. But he was telling about a friend of his, the friend of his life, his one dearest Friend. And when he remembers how they treated Him his eyes fill up, and his heart beats till it thumps, and his quill sticks into the paper in sheer reluctance to tell the story.

I think likely in the original manuscript, John's own first copy, the writing was a bit shaky and uneven here. The dew of his wet eyes drops and blurs the words a bit as he puts down, "He came to His own, and . . they who were His own . . received . . Him . . not."

One day a young student was crossing the quadrangles of one of the old Scottish Universities towards his quarters in the dormitory. He was not feeling well. His eyes had troubled him and made his work very difficult. On the advice of a friend he sought the judgment of an expert in the treatment of the eyes. The specialist made a very thorough examination and then informed the young student tactfully but plainly that he would lose his eyesight, surely and not slowly.

Lose his eyesight? A sudden terrific actual blow between his eyes could not have stunned his body more than this stunned brain and heart. Lose his eyesight! All his plans and coveted ambitions seemed slipping clean out from his grasp. With the loss of eyes would go the loss of university training, and so of all his dreams. Dazed, blinded, he groped his way rather than walked out of the physician's office.

His life was to be joined with another's. And now he turned his distracted steps towards her home, hungry doubtless for some word or touch of comfort for his sore heart. And he was thinking, too, that with this utter break-up of the future she must be told. And as he talked he said in quiet manly words that under these unexpected circumstances, and the radical change in his prospects, she must be free to do as she thought best.

And she took her freedom! Yet she was a woman. And a woman's mission is to teach man love by the real thing of love, by being it herself, and drawing it out into full flower in him. That was the second staggering blow. A second time he groped his dazed way out of the house, down the street, into his lone student quarters.

But another One was near, brooding over him, and tenderly holding his breaking heart, and speaking words of warm comfort, and breathing in the freshing breath of true love. And as he yielded to this it overcame all else. A new mood came and dominated. And it became the fixed thing mastering all his life. Now he sits down, and out of his torn bleeding but newly-touched heart writes the words we have all learned to sing:

And with but a single change, the change of a word or two in one line, they stand as at first written. I suppose his biographer omitted the incident for the same reason that the first three Gospels may have omitted the incident of Lazarus while he was still living. So there was a sheltering from personal embarrassment.

He came to his own and his own received him not. He—Jesus came to His own and they that were His own received Him not. Aye, there's more to add: He comes to His own—you and me—to-day. And His own—

You and I must finish that sentence, each in his own way. And we will; and we do. We may copy out in our lives just what these men of old did as told by John. Some of us do. We may do some fine revision work on the text of John's version as we translate it now into the experience of our own hearts, and into the life of our own lives. That's the only way to understand the next sentence about being taken into the family of God and sharing the fullness of life that is common there.

And this bit that is put down here is only a bit of copy work. These things are talked and written only that we may be given a lift into closer touch of heart and life with the Christ, the Son of God, and the Brother and Saviour of men.

II

The Wooing Lover
Who it Was that Came
—"The Hound of Heaven."

"Behold, I stand at the door and knock: if any man hear my voice and open the door, I will come in to him, and will sup with him, and he with me."
—Rev. iii. 20.

II

The Wooing Lover
(John i. 1-18.)
In His Own Image.
Love gives. It gives freely and without stint, yet always thoughtfully.
It gives itself out, its very life. This is its life, to give its life.
It lives most by giving most. So it comes into fullness of life.

So it gets. A thing of life, in its own image, comes walking eagerly with outstretched arms to its embrace. It gives that it may get. Yet the giving is the greater. It brings most joy.

This is the very essence of life, this giving creating spirit. It is everywhere, in lower life and higher and highest, wherever the touch of God has come. The sun gives itself out in life and light and warmth. And out to greet it comes a bit of itself—the fine form and sweet fragrance of the rose, the tender blade of grass, the unfolding green of the leaf, the wealth of the soil, the song of the bird and the grateful answer of all nature.

The hen sits long patient days on her nest. And forth comes cheeping life in her own image, answering the call of her mothering spirit. The mother-bird in the nest in the crotch of the tree gives her life day by day in brooding love. And her wee nestling offspring, in her own image, answers with glad increase of strength and growth.

Father and mother of our human kind give of their very life that new life may come. And under the overshadowing touch of an unseen Presence comes a new life made in their image, and in His who broods unseen over all three. And over the life wrecked by sin broods the Spirit of God. And out through the doorway of an opening will, comes a new creature of winsome life in the very image of that brooding Spirit of God.

This is the holy commonplace of all life. It is the touch of God. It is everywhere about us, and beneath and above. The father-mother Spirit of God broods over all our common life. And when things go wrong, He broods a bit closer and tenderer. He meets every need of the life He has created. And He meets it in the same way, by giving Himself.

And there's always the response. The fragrance of the rose answers the sun. The pipped shell brings the longed-for answer to the gladdened mother-bird. The ever wondrous babe-eyes give unspeakable answer to the yearning of father and mother heart. The heart of man leaps at the call of his God.

This makes quite clear the wondrous response men gave Jesus when He walked among us. Jesus was God coming a bit closer in His brooding love to mend a break and restore a blurred image. And men answered Him. They couldn't help it. How they came! They didn't understand Him, but they felt Him. They couldn't resist the tender, tremendous pull upon their hearts of His mere presence.

And Jesus drew man into the closest touch of intimate friendship. The long-range way of doing things never suited Him. And it doesn't. He didn't keep man at arm's length. And He doesn't. And then because they were friends, He and they, they were eager to serve, and willing even to suffer, to walk a red-marked roadway for Him they loved.

The Gospel According to—You.

Among all those who felt and answered the call of Jesus was one called John, John the disciple. Jesus drew John close. John came close. John lived close. John came early and he stayed late. He stayed to the very end, into the evening glow of life. And all his long life he was under the tender holy spell of Jesus' presence. He was swayed by the Jesus-passion. Always burning, he was yet never consumed; only the alloy burned up and burned out, himself refined to the quality of life called eternal.

Then John came to the end of his long life. And he knew he would be slipping the tether of life and going out and up and in to the real thing of life. And I think John was a bit troubled. Not because he was going to die. This never troubles the man who knows Jesus. The Jesus-touch overcomes the natural twinges of death. But he was troubled a bit in spirit for a little by the thought that he would not be on earth any longer to talk to people about Jesus. And to John this was the one thing worth while. This was the life-passion.

And so I think John prayed about it a bit. For this is what he did. He said to himself, "I will write a book. I'll make it a little book, so busy people can quickly read it. I'll pick out the simplest words I know so common folks everywhere that don't have dictionaries can easily understand. And I'll make them into the shortest simplest sentences I can so they can quickly get my story of Jesus." And so John wrote his little book. And we call it the story of Jesus according to John, or, as we commonly say the Gospel—the God-story—according to John.

And all this is a simple bit of a parable. It is a parable in action. Jesus is brooding over us, giving Himself, warmly wooing us. He woos us into personal friendship with Himself. And then He asks that each of us shall write a gospel. This is the Gospel according to John; and these others according to Luke and Mark and Matthew. He means that there shall be the gospel according to—you. What is your name? put it in there. Then you get the Master's plan. There is to be the gospel according to Charles and Robert and George, and Mary and Elizabeth and Margaret.

And you say, "Write a gospel? I couldn't do that. You don't mean that. That's just a bit of preaching." No, it isn't preaching. It's so. I do not mean to write with a common pen of steel or gold; nor on just common paper of rags or wood-pulp. But I do mean—He means—that you shall write with the pen of your daily life. And that you shall write on the paper of the lives of those you're touching and living with every day.

Clearly, He meant, and He means, that you and I shall live such simple unselfish lovable Jesus-touched lives, in just the daily commonplace round of life, that those we live with shall know the whole story of Jesus' love and life; His love burned out for us till there were no ashes, and His life poured out for us till not a red drop was left unspilled.

Are you writing your gospel? Is your life spelling out this simple wondrous God-story? I can find out, though, of course, I shall not. What I mean is this,—the crowd knows. The folks that touch you every day, they know. This old Bible was never printed so much as to-day, nor issued more numerously. And—thoughtfully—it was never read less by the common crowd on the common street of life than to-day.

That doesn't mean that the crowd doesn't read what it supposes to be religious literature. It does. I wish we church folk read our religious literature as faithfully as this crowd I speak of reads its. It is reading the gospel according to you, and reading it daily, and closely, and faithfully, and remembering what it reads, and being shaped by it.

This Bible I have here is bound in—I think it is called sealskin. I tried to get the best wearing binding I could. But I've discovered that there's a better binding than this. The best binding for the Gospel is shoe-leather. The old Gospel of the Son of God is at its best as it is being tramped out on the common street of life. Its truths stand out clearest as they're walked out. Its love comes warmest, its power is most resistless as it comes to you in the common give-and-take of daily touch in home and shop and street. Are you writing your copy of the Gospel?

You know that sometimes scholars have found some precious manuscripts in old monasteries. They have gone into some old, grey, stone monkery in the Near East, and they have run across old manuscripts hidden away in some dark cell, covered with dust and with rubbish, perhaps. With much tact and diplomacy they have at length managed to get possession of the coveted manuscript. And they have been fairly delighted to find that they have gotten hold of a remnant, a very precious remnant, of one of these Gospels. In just this way much invaluable light has been gotten that made possible these precious revised versions.

I wonder if your gospel—the one you're writing with your life—is just a remnant, a ragged remnant. And perhaps there's a good bit of dusting necessary, and removing of rubbish, to get even at what there is there. And some of the shy hungry hearts that touch you and me need to use quite a bit of unconscious diplomacy perhaps to get even as much as they do. I wonder. The crowd knows. It could throw a good bit of light here. How much of this old Jesus-story are you really living!

Of course, there's a special touch of inspiration in these four Gospels. The Holy Spirit brooded over these men in a special way as they wrote. That is true. These are the standard Gospels. We would never know the blessed story but for these four Spirit-breathed little books. But it is also true that that same Holy Spirit will guide you in the writing of your version of the Gospel.

These four Gospels are different from each other. The colouring of Luke's warm personality, and of his physician habit of thought is in his Gospel very plainly. And so it is with each one of these Gospels. And, even so, there will be the colouring of your personality, your habit of thought, the distinct tinge of the experience you have been through, in the gospel you write with the pen of your life, and bind up in the shoe-leather of your daily round.

But through all of this there will be the simple, subtle, but very real, atmosphere of the Holy Spirit, helping you make the story plain and full, and helping people to understand that story as it is lived, as they never can simply by hearing it told with tongues or read through eyes.

Are you writing your gospel? Is your daily life spelling out the life and love of Jesus, that life that was poured out till none was left, that love that was burned out till even the ashes were burned up, too? This is the Master's plan. And practically it is the crowd's only chance.

God in Human Garb.

Now I want to have you turn with me to the opening lines of John's Gospel. There are not many of these opening lines. The whole story is a short one. These lines at the beginning are like an etching, there are the fewest touches of pen on paper, of black ink on white surface. But the few lines are put in so simply and skilfully that they make an exquisite picture. It's the picture of God coming in human garb as a wooing Lover.

I think it might be best perhaps if I might simply give you a sort of free reading of these opening lines, with a word of comment or illustration to try to make the meaning simpler. It will be a putting of John's words into the simple every-day colloquial speech that we English-speaking people use. John used very simple language in his own telling of the story in his mother-tongue. And it may help if we try to do the same.

You will quickly see how very simple this free translation will be. Yet, let me say, that though homely and simple it will be strictly accurate to what John is thinking and saying in his own native speech. I mean of course, so far as I can find out just what he is thinking and saying.

Let us turn then to John's Gospel, at its beginning. And it will help very much if we keep our Bibles open as we talk and read together.

Listen: in the beginning there was a wondrous One. He was the mind of God thinking out to man. He was the heart of God throbbing love out to man's heart. He was the face of God looking into man's face. He was the voice of God, soft and low, clear and distinct, speaking into man's ears. He was the hand of God, strong and tender, reaching down to take man by the hand and lead him back to the old trysting-place under the tree of life, down by the river of water of life.

He was the person of God wearing a human coat and human shoes, hand-pegged, walking in freely amongst us that we might get our tangled up ideas about God and ourselves and about life untangled, straightened out. He was God Himself wrapped up in human form coming close that we might get acquainted with Him all over again.

This is part of the meaning of the little five-lettered word in his own tongue that John chooses and uses, at the first here, as a new name for Him who was commonly called Jesus. It was because of our ears that he used the new word. If he had said "Jesus" at once, they would have said "Oh! yes, we know about Him." And at once their ears would have gone shut to the thing that John is saying.

For they didn't know. And we don't. We know words. The thing, the real thing, we know so little. So John uses a new word at the first, and so floods in new light. And then we come to see whom he is talking about. It's a bit of the diplomacy of God so as to get in through dulled ears and truth-hardened minds down in to the heart.

Nature always seems eager to meet a defect. It seems to hurry eagerly forward to overcome defects and difficulties. The blind man has more acute hearing and a more delicate sense of feel. The deaf man's eyes grow quicker to watch faces and movements and so learn what his ears fail to tell him. The lame man leans more on other muscles, and they answer with greater strength to meet the defect of the weaker muscles.

The bat has shunned the light so long through so many bat-generations that it has become blind, but it has remarkable ears, and nature has grown for it an abnormal sense of touch, and a peculiar sensitiveness even where there is no contact, so that it avoids obstacles in flying with a skill that seems uncanny, incredulous.

I remember in Cincinnati one night, sitting on the platform of a public meeting by the side of a widely known Christian worker and speaker who was blind. As various men spoke he quietly made brief comments to me,—" He doesn't strike fire." And then, "He doesn't touch them." And then, "Ah! he's got them; that's it; now they're burning." And it was exactly so as he said. I sat fascinated as I watched the crowd and heard his comments. The sense of discerning what was going on in another way than by sight had been grown in him by the very necessity of his blindness. Defect in one sense was overcome by nature, by increase in another sense.

When Queen Victoria was in residence in Scotland at Balmoral it was her kindly custom to present the various clergymen who preached in the Castle chapel with a photograph marked with her autograph. When George Matheson, the famous blind preacher, came she showed the fine thoughtful tact for which she was famous. Clearly an autographed photograph would not mean much in itself to a blind man. So the Queen had a miniature bust-statue made and presented to him as her acknowledgment of his service. And so where his eyes failed to let him see, his sense of touch would carry to his mind and heart the fine features of the gracious sovereign he was so glad to serve.

Jesus was God coming in such a way that we could know Him by the feel. We had gone blind to His face. We couldn't read His signature plainly autographed by His own hand on the blue above and the brown below. But when Jesus came men knew God by the feel. They didn't understand Jesus. But the sore hungry crowds reached out groping trembling fingers, and they knew Him. They began to get acquainted with their gracious Sovereign.

All this gives the simple clue to this word "Word" which John uses as a new name for Jesus. Man had grown deaf to the music of God's voice, blind to the beauty of His face, slow-hearted to the pleading of His presence. His hand was touching us but we didn't feel it. So He came in a new way, in a very homely close-up way and walked down our street into our own doors that we might be caught by the beauty of His face, and thrilled by the music of His voice, and thralled by the spell of His presence.

God at His Best.

John goes on: and this wondrous One was with God. There were two of them. And the two were together. They were companions, they were friends, fellows together. And this One was God. Each was the same as the other. This is the same One who was in the later creative beginning with God. It was through this One that all things were made. And, of all things that have been made, not any thing was made without Him.

You remember that John's Gospel and Genesis begin in the same way,—"in the beginning." But John's "in the beginning," the first one, is not the same as the Genesis "in the beginning." John's is the beginning before there was any beginning. It is the beginning before they had begun making calendars on the earth, because there wasn't any earth yet to make calendars on. Then this second time the phrase is used John comes to the later creative beginning with which Genesis opens. This is what John is saying here.

"In Him was life." Out of Him came life. Out of Him comes life. There was no life, there is none, except what was in this One, and what came, and comes out from Him all the time. How patient God is! There walks a man down the street. He leaves God out of his life. He may remember Him so far as to use His name blasphemously to punctuate and emphasize what he is saying. Yonder walks a woman in the shadow of the street at night. And her whole life is spent walking in the dark shadow of the street of life. And her whole life is a blasphemy against her personality, and against the God who gave her that precious sacred personality.

Take these two as extreme illustrations. There is life there; life of the body, of the mind, life of the human spirit. Listen softly, all the life there is there, is coming out all the time from this One of whom John is talking. It is not given once as a thing to be taken and stored. It is being given. It is coming constantly with each breath, from this wondrous One. This is what John is saying here.

How patient God is! Only we don't know what patience is. We know the word, the label put on the outside. We don't know the thing, except sometimes in very smallest part. For patience is love at its best. Patience is God at His strongest and tenderest and best.

I think likely when we get up yonder, we'll stop one another on the golden streets. There'll be a hand put out, gripping the other hard. And we'll look into each other's eyes with our eyes big. And we'll say with breaking voices, "How patient God was with us down there on the earth, down there in London and New York."

In Him was life. Out of His hand and heart is coming to us all the time all we are and all we have. We may leave God practically out. So many of us do. But He never leaves us out. The creating, sustaining touch of His Hand is ever upon each of us, upon all the world.

Though He cannot do all for us He would except as we gladly come and let Him. What He is giving us is so much. It's our all. Yet it is the smaller part. There's the fuller part. This is the whole drive of John's story, this fuller part. Out of Him Jesus, into us will come the newer, the better, the abundant quality of life, if He may have His way.

And John adds,—"and the life was the light of men." He was what we have. He gives Himself; not things, but a person. With God everything is personal. We men go to the impersonal so much, or we try to. We do our best at it. We have a great genius for organization, especially in this western half of the earth.

As I came back from a four years' absence from my own country, I was instantly conscious of a change. Either my ears were changed or things about me were. I think likely both. But the wheels were going faster than ever. There were more wheels, and their whir seemed never out of ear-shot. Commercial wheels, and educational, philanthropic and religious, political and humanitarian, thicker and faster than ever, driving all day, and with almost no night there.

And the whole attempt is to make the machine do the thing with as little dependence as possible on the human element, even though the human element was never emphasized more. Contradictory? Yet there it is. We men go to the _im_personal. Yet deep down in our hearts we hunger for the human touch, the warm personal touch. This after all is the thing. We all feel that. Yet the whole crowding of life's action is to crowd it out.

But with God everything is personal. The life is the light of men. What He is in Himself—that is what He gives. And this is all the light and life we ever have. Men make botany. God makes flowers breathing their freshening fragrance noiselessly up into your face. Man makes astronomy. God makes the stars, shaking their firelight out of the blue down into your wondering eyes on a clear moonless night. Man makes theology. And theology has its place, when it's kept in its place. God gives us Jesus.

I don't know much about botany. My knowledge of astronomy is very limited. And the more I read of theology, whether Western or Eastern, Latin Church or Greek, the first Seven Councils or the later ones, the more I stand perplexed. It's a thing fearsomely and wonderfully manufactured, this theology. But I frankly confess to a great fondness for flowers, and for stars, and a love for Jesus that deepens ever more in reverential awe and in tenderness and grateful devotion. The life was the light of men. He Himself is all that we have. We go to things. We reckon worth and wealth by things. He gives Himself. And He asks, not things, but one's self.

Packing Most in Least.

And John goes quietly on with his great simple story: "and the light shineth in the darkness," John has a way of packing much in little. Here he packs four thousand years into three English letters. For he has been back in that creative Genesis week. And now with one long stride he puts his foot down in the days when Jesus walks among us as a man. Forty centuries, by the common reckoning, packed into three letters e-t-h. Rather a skilful bit of packing that. Yet it is not unusual. It is characteristic both of John and of the One that guides John's pen. When He is allowed to have free sway the Holy Spirit packs much in little.

That rugged old Hebrew prophet of fire and storm, Elijah, standing in the grey dawn, in the mouth of an Arabian cave, had the whole of a new God—a God of tender gentle love—packed into an exquisite sound of gentle stillness, that smote so subtly on his ear, and completely melted and changed this man of rock and thunder. It's a new man that turns his face north again. The new God that had compacted Himself anew inside the ruggedly faithful old man is revealed in the prophet's successor. This is the new spirit, so unlike the old Elijah, that comes as a birth-right heritage upon young Elisha. Great packing work that.

That fine-grained young university fellow on the Damascus road, driving hard in pursuit of his earnest purpose, had the whole of a God, a new God to him, packed into a single flash of blinding light out of the upper blue. He had the whole of a new plan, an utterly changed plan for his life, packed into a single sentence spoken into his amazed ears as he lies in the dust.

And if this Holy Spirit may have His way—a big if? Yes: yet not too big to be gotten rid of at once: God puts in the if's, that we may get the strength of choosing. We put them out, if we do. If He may have His way He'll pack—listen quietly, with your heart—He'll pack the whole of a Jesus inside you and me. Much in little! Most in least! And the more we let Him in, the bigger that "most" prints itself to our eyes, and the more that "least" dwindles down to the disappearing point.

God gives us His own self in Jesus. Jesus comes to live inside of us. He doesn't give us things, but Himself. We talk about salvation. There's something better—a Saviour. We talk about help in trouble. There's something immensely more—a Friend, alongside, close up. We talk about healing—sometimes, not so much these days; the subject is so much confused. There's something much better—a Healer, living within, whose presence means healing and health for body and spirit.

Then John says, "the light shineth in the darkness." This is God's way of treating darkness. There are two ways of treating darkness, man's and God's. Man's way is to attack the darkness. Suppose this hall where we are were quite dark, all shuttered up, and suppose we were new on the earth, and not familiar with darkness. We want to hold a meeting. But how shall we get rid of this strange darkness that has come down over everything? Let's each of us get a bucket or pail or basin, and take some of the darkness out. So we'll get rid of it, and its inconvenience.

And if the suggestion were made seriously there might be talk of putting the suggestor in a certain sort of institution for the safety of the community. Yet this is the way we go at the other darkness, the worse moral darkness.

God's way is quite different; indeed just the exact reverse let the light shine. The darkness can't stand the light. If the hall were quite dark, and I scratched only a parlour-match, instantly as the little flame broke out of the end of the stick some of the darkness would go. It's surprising how much would go, and how quickly. The darkness can't stand the light. It flees like a hunted hare before a pack of hounds.

There may be times when action must betaken by a community against certain forms of evil, so damnable, and so strongly entrenched, and so threatening to the purity of home and young and of all. But note keenly that this is incidental. It is immensely important at times, but it is distinctly secondary. The great simple plan of God is this: let the light shine. The darkness flees like a whipped cur, tail tightly curled down and in, before the real thing of light.

Let me ask you a question. Come up a bit closer and listen quietly, for this is tremendously serious. And it's the quietest spoken word that reaches the inner cockles of the heart. Listen: is it a bit dark down where you live? Morally dark? Spiritually? How about that? in commercial circles and social and fraternal, in church and home and city and neighbourhood. Is it a bit dark? Or, have I found the Garden of Eden at last before the serpent entered?

Because if it be a bit dark, softly, please, let me say it very quietly, for it may sound critical, and I would not have that for anything. We are talking only to help. Though sometimes the truth itself does have a merciless edge. If it be a bit dark does it not suggest that the light has not been shining as it was meant to? For where the light shines the darkness goes.

For, you see, this is still God's plan for treating darkness. It is meant to be true to-day of each of us,—"the light shineth in the darkness." Of course, we are not the light. He is the Light. But we are the light-holders. I carry the Light of the world around inside of me. And so do you, if you do. It is not because of the "me," of course, but because of the great patience and faithfulness of Him who is the Light. A very rickety cheap lantern may carry a clear light, and the man in the ditch find good footing in the road again.

You and I are meant to be the human lanterns carrying the Light, and letting it shine clearly fully out. And you know when some one else is providing the light the chief thing about the lantern is that the glass of the lantern be kept clean and clear so the light within can get freely out. The great thing is that we shall live clean transparent lives so the Light within may shine clearly out. We may live unselfish clean Christly lives, by His great grace. And through that kind of lives, the Light itself shines out, and shines out most, and most clearly.

Over at the mouth of the Hudson, where I call it home, there are some strange things seen. Sometimes the glass of this human lantern gets smoky, badly smoked. And sometimes it even gets cobwebby, rather thickly covered up. And even this has been known to happen up there,— it'll seem very strange to you people doubtless—this; they write finely phrased essays on the delicate shading of grey in the smoke on the glass of the human lantern.

They meet together and listen to essays, in rarely polished English, on the exquisite lace-like tracery of the cobwebs on the glass of the human lantern. But look! Hold your heart still and look! There's the crowd in the road in the dark, struggling, jostling, stumbling, and falling into the ditch at the side of the road, ditched and badly mired, because the light hasn't gotten to them. The Light's there. It's burning itself out in passionate eagerness to help. But the human lanterns are in bad shape.

"Rhetoric!" do you say? I wish it were. I wish with my heart it were. Look at the crowds for yourself. There they go down the street, pell-mell, bewildered, blinded, some of them by will-o'-the-wisp lights, ditched and mired many of them. The thing is only too terribly true.

Our Lord's great plan, bearing the stamp of its divinity in its sheer human simplicity, is this: we who know Jesus are to live Him. We're to let the whole of a Jesus, crucified, risen, living, shine out of the whole of our lives.

Is it a bit dark down where you are? Let the Light shine. Let the clear sweet steady Jesus-light shine out through your true clean quiet Jesus-swayed and Jesus-controlled life. Then the darkness must go. It can't stand the Light. It can't withstand the purity and insistence of its clear steady shining. And the darkness will go: slowly, reluctantly, angrily, doggedly, making hideous growling noises sometimes, raising the dust sometimes, but it will go. It must go before the Light. The Light's resistless. This is our Lord's wondrous plan through His own, and His irresistible plan for the crowd, and His plan against the prince of darkness.

The Heart-road to the Head.

Then John goes on to say, "the darkness apprehended it not." The old common version says "comprehended"; the revisions, both English and American, say "apprehended." Both are rather large words, larger in English than John would use. John loved to use simple talk. Yet there's help even in these English words. Comprehend is a mental word. It means to take hold of with your mind; to understand. Apprehend is a physical word. It means to take hold of with your hand.

You can't comprehend Jesus. That is just the simple plain fact. You may have a fine mind. It may be well schooled and trained. You may have dug into all the books on the subject, English and German and the few French. You may have spent a lifetime at it. But at the end there is immensely more of Jesus that you don't understand than the part that you do understand. You've touched the smaller part only, just the edges. You cannot take Jesus in with your mind simply.

The one is too big and the other too limited for that particular process.

But, listen with your heart, you can apprehend Him. You can take hold of Him. There isn't one of us here, however poorly equipped mentally and in training, and too busy with life's common duties to get much time for reading, not one of us, who may not reach out your hand, the hand of your heart, the hand of your life, the hand of your simple childlike trust—if you're great enough in simplicity to be childlike, to be natural, not one of us, but may reach out the hand and take in all there is of Jesus.

And the striking thing to mark is this, that we don't really begin to comprehend until we apprehend. Only as we take Him into heart and life can we really understand. It's as if the heat in the heart made by His presence there loosens up the grey juices of your brain, and it begins to work freely and clearly.

Of course, this is a commonplace in the educational world. It is well understood there that no student does his best work, no matter what that work may be, in science or philosophy or in mathematics or in laboratorial research, his mind cannot do its best, or be at its best, until his heart has been kindled by some noble passion. The key to the life is in the heart, that is the emotions and purposes tied together. The approach to the mind is through the heart. The fire of pure emotion and of noble purpose burning together, works out through the mind into the life. This is nature's order.

But what John is saying here, put into as simple language as he would use, is this: "the darkness wouldn't let the light in, and couldn't shut it out, and couldn't dull the brightness of its shining." It tried. It tried first at Bethlehem. The first spilling of blood came there. There was the shedding of blood at both ends of Jesus' career, and innocent blood each time. It tried at the Nazareth precipice, and in the spirit-racking wilderness. It tried by stones, then in Gethsemane, then at Calvary.

And there it seemed to have succeeded. At last the light was shut in and down; the door was shut and barred and bolted. And I suppose there was great glee in the headquarters of darkness. But the Third Morning came. And the bars of darkness were broken, as a woman breaks the sewing-cotton at the end of the seam. The Light could not be held down by darkness. It broke out more brightly than ever. The darkness couldn't shut the light out. And it can't.

Let the light shine. Let it shine out through the clear clean glass of an unselfish, Jesus-cleansed Jesus-fired life lived for Him in the commonplace round, and the shut-away corner. And the darkness will go. The darkness cannot shut out the light, nor keep it down, nor resist the gentle resistless power of its soft clear flooding. Let the Light shine down in that corner where you are. And the darkness, darkness that can be felt, and is felt so sorely deep down in your spirit, in its uncanny Egyptian blackness, that darkness will break, and more, clear, and go, go, go, till it's clear gone.

And so ends John's first great paragraph. It is so tremendous in its simplicity that, Greek-like, men stumble over its simple tremendousness. Away back in the beginning God revealed Himself in making a home for man, and in bringing the man, made in His own image, to his home. And then when the damp unwholesome darkness came stealing in swamping the home and man He came Himself, flooding in the soft clear pure light of His presence, to free man from the darkness and woo him out into the light.

Tarshish or Nineveh?

Then John goes on into his second paragraph. "There came a man, sent from God, whose name was John." Why? Because man was in the dark. He sent a man to help a man. He used a man to reach a man. He always does. Run clear through this old Book of God, and then clear through that other Book of God—the book of life, and note that this is God's habit. He, Himself, uses the path He had made for human feet. With greatest reverence let it be said that God must use a human pathway for His feet.

Even when He would redeem a world He came, He must needs come, as a Man, one of ourselves. He touches men through men. The pathway of His helping feet is always a common human pathway. And, will you mark keenly that the highest level any life ever reaches, or can reach, is this: to be a pathway for the feet of a wooing winning God.

And this is still true. It is meant to be true to-day that there came a man, sent from God, whose name is—your name. You put in your own name in that sentence, then you get God's plan for you. For as surely as this particular John of the desert and of the plain living, and the burning speech, was sent by God, so surely is every man of us a man sent by God on some particular errand. And the greatest achievement of life is to find and fit into the plan of God for one's life. This is the only great thing one can do. Anything else is merely labelled "great." And that label washes off. This is the one thing worth while.

The bother is we don't always get the verbs, the action words, of that sentence straight. John was a man sent from God. And he came. All men are sent But they don't all come, some go; go their own way. There was a man sent from God whose name was Jonah. But he didn't come. He went. He was sent to Nineveh on the extreme east. He went towards Tarshish on the extreme west; just the opposite direction. Every man is headed either for Nineveh or Tarshish, God's way or his own. Which way are you headed?

Some of us go to Tarshish religiously. We go our own way, and sing hymns and pray, to make it seem right and keep from hearing the inner voice. We hold meetings at the boat-wharf, while waiting for the Tarshish ship to lift anchor. We have services in the steerage and second-class and distribute tracts and New Testaments; but all the time we're headed for Tarshish; our way, not God's. It won't do simply to do good. We must do God's will. Find that and fit into it.

The meetings and tracts are only good but they ought to be on the train to Nineveh, and in Nineveh where God's sent you. Are you berthed on the boat for Tarshish? or have you a seat engaged on the train for Nineveh? going your own way? or God's? John was sent and he came. You and I are sent. Are we coming or going? coming God's way? or, going our own?

Living Martyrs.

This true-hearted burning man of the deserts came for a witness. Here we strike one of John's great words. You remember the three things that witness means? that you know something; that you tell what you know; and that you tell it most with your life. And telling it with your life means, not only by the way you live, but, too, even though the telling of it may cost you your life. It came to mean all of that with this witness.

It came to mean that with a new fullness of meaning, a peculiar significance, to the great Witness, of whom John told. This was the very throbbing heart of the wooing errand. This explains the tenderness and tenacity of the Lover in His wooing in the midst of intensest opposition, and in spite of it.

The opposition brought about the terrific grouping of circumstances which the great Lover-witness used as the tremendous climax of both wooing and witnessing. No one doubts the reality of Jesus' witness to the Father's love before men. And no one, who has had any touch at all with Him, doubts the tremendous pull upon one's heart of such a wooing appeal as that Calvary climax of witnessing made, and makes.

And this, mark it keenly, is still the plan. "The-same-came-for-witness" is meant to be true of each follower of the Christ. This is to be the dominant underchording of all our lives. This is to be the never-absent motive gripping us, and our possessions and our plans. The rest is incidental in a true life.

It may be a "rest" that takes most of the waking hours with most of us, most of our strength and thought. But there's an undercurrent in every life. And the undercurrent is the controlling current. It makes us what we really are. It may be quite different from the upper current controlled by the outer necessities of circumstances. And with the true Jesus-man this is the undercurrent, this thing of witnessing.

Do you know something of Jesus? Do you know the cleansing of His blood? Do you know the music of His peace in your heart? Do you know a bit of the subtle fragrance of His presence? Do you know the power of His Name when temptations come, when the road gets slippery, and your feet go out from under you—almost. Then His Name, its power, and you hold steady. Do you know something about such things?

Then tell it. This is the plan—telling. It's a Gospel of telling. Tell it with your lips tactfully, gently, boldly, earnestly. But tell it far more, and most with your life. Let what you are, when you're not thinking about this sort of thing, let that tell it. That's the greatest telling, the best.

And, softly, now, when you get to the end of telling what you know, listen quietly, don't go to digging into books for something to tell your class or the meeting or the crowd. Don't do that. Books have their place, good books, but it's always a sharply secondary place, or third, or lower down yet. Poor crowd that must be fed on retailed books worked over! Don't do that. Know more. Know Jesus better. Trust Him more fully. Risk more on following where He clearly leads. Then you can tell more and better.

Sometimes I'm asked, "How can I have more faith?" Well, not by thinking about your faith. Not by books or definitions chiefly, however they may help some. I can tell you how: Follow where the Master's quiet voice is clearly calling. Go where it is plain to you that that pierced hand is leading.

"Ah! but the way is a bit narrow," you think. "And it's steep. There are sharp-edged stones under foot. And those bushes are growing rank on both sides narrowing the path. And thorns scratch and hurt and sting. This other road where I am now—this is a good Christian road. My

Christian brothers are here. I'd rather stay here."

And so you stay. You don't say "no" to the calling voice. You simply act "no." No wonder you get confused and tangled. It's only in the path of following clear leading that there comes sweetest peace, with no nagging doubts and mental confusion. There only will you have more faith, know more of Him, touch with whom is the realest faith. And so only will the witness be told out to the crowd on the street of your life, of the power and satisfying peace of this Jesus.

This is the witnessing we're sent to do. And the crowds crowd to listen, when it's given. This is the way the Witness did. He followed the clear Father-voice, though the road led straight across the regular roads through thorn hedges and thick underbrush. Should not the servant tread it still?

The word that John uses here underneath our English word witness is the word from which our English word martyr comes. And martyr has come to mean one who gives his life clear out in a violent way for the truth he believes. But, do you know, that is easy. "Easy?" You say, "Surely not, you're certainly wrong there." No, you are right. It is not easy. To face a storm of lead, or feel the sharp-edged blade, or yield to the eating flame,—that is never easy.

But this is what I mean. There's the heroic in it, and that helps. You brace yourself for it. The terrible crisis comes. You pull together and pray and resolutely, desperately, face it. A little while, and it's over. You've been true in the sharp crisis. You have taken a place with the noble army of martyrs. And we who hear of it have a martyr's halo about your head.

But there's something immensely harder to do. Without making a whit less than it is the splendid courage of martyrdom, there's something that takes immensely more courage, and a deeper longer-seasoned heroism, and that is to be a living martyr, to bear the simple true witness tactfully but clearly, when it takes the very life of your life to do it, though it doesn't take your bodily life in a violent way.

You know they don't martyr people these days for their Christian faith. At least not in the western half of the earth, the Christian hemisphere. No, that's quite behind the calendar. That's rather crude, quite behind the cultured advanced Christian progress of our day. Our Christian civilization has gone long strides beyond that. We have grown much more refined. Now we kill them socially. Many a one who would live true to the Jesus-ideals in daily life in a simple sane way finds certain social doors shut and carefully barred.

We kill them commercially now. The man who will quietly hew to the Jesus-line in business is quite apt to find his income reduced. The bulk of business shrinks. The thermometer is run down below the living point. We kill men by frost now. The blockade system is skilfully used; isolation and insulation from certain circles. We are much more refined.

The great need to-day is of living witnesses to the Christ in home, and social circle, in the street, and in the market-place.

The Forgotten Preacher.

With a simplicity in sticking to his main point, John goes quietly on: "that he might be a witness of the light." That's rather interesting. It was of the light he was to bear witness; not of himself. It was not the technical accuracy of his work, not its scholarliness and skill that absorbed him, but that the crowd got the light. Rather striking that, when you break away from the atmosphere round about, and think into it a bit.

Here's a man walking down a country road. It's a hot day. The road's dusty. He gets a bit weary and thirsty. He comes across a bit of a spring by the side of the road. Clear cool water it is. And some one has thoughtfully left a tin-cup on a ledge of rock near by. And the man gratefully drinks and goes on his way refreshed. He quite forgets the tin-cup.

Sometimes the tin-cup seems to require much attention, up in the corner of the world where my tent is pitched. It has to be handled very carefully and considerately if one is to get what possible drops of water it may contain. The human tin-cup seems to bulk very big in the drinking process, sometimes, in my corner of the planet. It is silver-plated sometimes; just common tin under the plating. There's some fine engraving on the silver-plating, noble sentiment, deftly expressed, and done in the engraver's best style. But the water is apt to be scanty, the drops rather few, in this sort of tin-cup. It's a bit droughty.

And sometimes even this has been known to occur: they have associations of these human tin-cups for self-admiration and other cultural purposes. And they have highly satisfactory meetings. But meanwhile, ah! look! hold still your heart, and look here. There's the crowd on the street, hot dusty street, exhausted, actually fainting for want of water, just good plain water of life. But there's none to be had; only tin-cups! John was eager to have men get a good drink. He was content as he watched them drink, and their eyes lighten. He was discontent and restless with anything else or less.

Do you remember the greatest compliment ever paid John, John the Herald? John was a great preacher. He had great drawing power. To-day we commonly go where people are hoping they'll stay while we talk to them. But John did otherwise. He went down to the Jordan bottoms, where the spirit ventilation was better, and called the people to him. And they came. They came from all over the nation, of every class. Literally thousands gathered to hear John. He had great drawing power.

And then something happened. Here is John to-day talking earnestly to great crowds down by the river-road. And here he is again to-morrow; but where are the crowds? John has lost his crowd. Same pulpit out in the open air, same preacher, same simple intense message burning in his heart, but—no congregation! The crowd's gone. Poor John! You must feel pretty bad. It's hard enough to fail, but how much harder after succeeding. Poor John, I'm so sorry for you.

But if you get close enough to John to see into his eye you quit talking like that. And if you get near enough to hear you find your sympathy is not needed. For John's eye is ablaze with a tender light, and the sound of an inner heart music reaches your ear as you get near him. And if you follow, as you instinctively do, the line of the light in his eye you quickly look down the road.

Oh! There's John's crowd. _They're listening to Jesus._ John's crowd has left him for his Master. And the forgotten preacher is the finest evidence of the faithfulness of the preacher. The crowd's getting the water, sweet cool refreshing water of life, direct from the fountain. They've clean forgotten the faithful common tin-cup. And John's so glad. John came that he might bear witness of the light. And he did. And the crowd heard. And they flocked to the light.

Here's a man preaching. And the people are listening. The benediction is pronounced. And they go out. And as they move slowly out they're talking, always talking. We don't seem yet to have demitted our privilege of talking after service. Here are two. Listen to them. "Isn't he a great preacher? so scholarly, so eloquent, so polished; and all those classical allusions. I didn't understand half he said; he certainly is a great preacher. We're very fortunate in such a man."

And the preacher, whoever he be, may know this for a bit of the certainty that occasionally will sift in. He may be a scholar. I wouldn't question it. And a polished orator. I wouldn't question that. But in the main thing, the one thing he's for, as a Jesus-witness, he is a splendid scholarly polished failure. Men are talking about him.

They've forgotten his Master, if indeed—ah, yes, if indeed he have a Master! He has a Saviour, let us earnestly hope, and willingly believe. But a Master! One that sweeps and sways his mind and culture and life like the strong wind sweeps the thin young saplings in the storm—clearly he knows nothing of that. Men are talking of him.

And here's another talking a bit It may be just a simple homely talk. Or he may likewise be scholarly and eloquent. A man should bring his best. The old classic is beaten oil for the lamps of the sanctuary. But there's the soft burning fire of the real thing in his message. And the people feel it. The air seems a-thrill with its quiet tensity. And the last amen is said. And again they go out.

And here are two walking down the road together, and as they come to the cross-street, one says to his companion, "Excuse me, please, I have to go down this way." And the "have-to" is the have-to of an intense desire to get off alone. And as he goes down the side street he's talking, but—to himself. Listen to him: "I'm not the man I ought to be, I wonder if Jesus is really like he said. I wonder if the thing's really so. I believe—yes, I really think I'll risk it. My life isn't like it should be. I'll risk trying this Jesus-way. I'll do it."

The man's clean forgotten the speaker. Oh, yes, he remembers the tone of the voice, and the look of the face, but indistinctly, far away. He's face-to-face with Jesus! And the forgotten speaker is the finest evidence of the faithfulness of his speaking. He is holding up the light. And men run into the light. They've clean forgot the little tin candlestick, they are so taken up with the light it holds.

The One Thing to Aim At.

And John keeps driving in on the point in his mind: "that all might believe through Him"; that they might listen, stop to think, agree as to the thing being believable, then trust it; then trust Him, the Light, risk something, risk, themselves to Him, then love, love with a passionate devotion. This was John's objective. It was the bull's-eye of his target never out of his keen Spirit-opened eye. Nothing else figured in.

This is the thing in all our living and serving and doing and giving, that men may know Jesus to the trusting, risking, loving point, the glad point. Everything that we can bring of gold and learning and labour and skill is precious, it is as purest gold, if it lead men into heart-touch with Jesus. And it clean misses the mark if it does less.

Who would be content to give a Belgian or Polish starveling a bare bit of bread, and a lonely stick of wood, and a rag of cloth. Bite and stick and cloth are good, but it's a meal and a fire, and some clothing, the man wants. And you have both ready at hand. Things are good, provided by money and skill and research and painstaking efforts. They do good. But it's Jesus men need. It's the warm touch that lets Him fully in with all of His human sympathy and all of His God-power, that's what they need.

Given the sun and quickly come warmth and food and shelter, health and vigour and increase of life. Given Jesus, and the warm touch with Him, in His simple fullness, just as He is, and surely and not slowly, there come flooding in all the rest of an abundant life, physical and mental and of the spirit.

John "was not the light." He was only the candlestick. And he was content to be that. He was a good candlestick. The light was held up. It could shine out. How grateful the crowd was. The road had been so dark. It is a bad thing when light and candlestick change places. The crowd seems to get the two confused sometimes. We get to thinking that the candlestick is the light, and the light is—lost sight of. We gather about the candlestick. It'll surely lead the way out through the dark night into day. It's such a good candlestick, so highly polished. And sometimes the human candlestick itself gets things a bit mixed. It thinks, then it feels, then it knows, with a peculiar quality of self-assertive certainty, that after all it is the light that lighteth every one that is so blessed as to come within the radius of its shining. And brass does take a high polish, and makes an attractive appearance. It does send out a sparkle and radiance if only it is somewhere within range of some real light, patient enough to keep on shining in the dark, regardless of non-appreciation or misrepresentation or misunderstanding.

Is it any wonder the road is so full of people wandering in the night gathered about candlesticks? Is it surprising that the ditches are so full of men and candlesticks mixed up and mired up together? Yet it is always heart-breaking. There may be talent and training of the highest and best, and scholarship and culture, eloquence and skill, institutions and philanthropies. And there is so much of these. And these are good in themselves, and of priceless practical worth when seen and held in their right relation to the thing.

But it needs to be said often and earnestly: these are not the light. They are given to point men better to the Light. They're road-signs, index-fingers. And they are seen at their best when they point to the Light so clearly that the crowd quite forgets them in hastening to the Light they point out. They serve their true purpose in being so forgotten. They are still serving and serving best even while forgotten.

The Real Thing of Light.

And John goes on to intensify yet more what he is thinking and saying: there was the true light, the real thing of light. They were bothered, in John's old age when he is writing, with false lights, make-pretend lights, that led people astray. Every generation seems to have been so bothered and confused. And even our own doesn't seem to have entirely escaped the subtle contagion. The ground is a bit swampy in places, boggy.

Low-lying land runs to bog and swamp. And the air gets thick with heavy vapours. And strange will-of-the-wisp lights form out of the foul damp gasses, and they flit about in the gloom this way and that. And people are led astray by them deeper into swamp and bog. It's surprising to find how many, that grow up in well-lit neighbourhoods, wander off after the swamp lights, and even follow them so contentedly. That's partly due, without doubt, to the false lights borrowing so much of the mere outer incidentals from the true. And they succeed in producing a make-up that easily deceives the unwary and untaught.

There's a teaching to-day, for instance, that magnifies bodily healing.
The name of Christ is freely used. And the old Book of God freely
quoted. And men are really healed. There can be no question of that.
There are sufficient facts at hand to make that incontestably clear.

But bodily healing does not necessarily argue divine power. There are results secured through the operation of unfamiliar mental powers that seem miraculous. And clearly there are devilish miracles as well as divine. Miracles simply reveal a supernatural power, that is, a power above the ordinary workings of nature. Then one must apply a touchstone, a test, to learn what that power is.

It is striking that in this teaching I speak of now there is never mention of the atoning blood of Christ. And this is the sure touchstone by which to detect the real thing of light and the make-believe. The outstanding thing in the life of Christ is His death, and the tremendous meaning which His own teaching put into that fact of His death.

There is none of the red tinge to this make-believe light. It has the unwholesome unnatural tingeing of swamp lights. And those who are healed through this teaching will find themselves in a bondage the more terrible because so subtle. And only the power of the blood of Christ can ever break that bondage.

There was the real thing of light. Here is the real thing of light. There's a distinct tingeing of red in it. It's the only light. It only is the light. Every other is a make-pretend light, however subtle its imitations and reflections: it will lead only into swamp and bog and ditch and worse.

And then John goes on to add a very simple bit that has not always been quite understood in its simplicity. There was the real thing of light that lighteth every man that cometh into the world. There is a little group of varied readings into the English here, found in the margin of the various revisions. But the central statement remains the same. Whether John is saying that the light, that lighteth every man, was now coming down into the world in a closer way. Or, that every man is lighted as he comes into the world, the chief thing being told is the same. Every man in the world is lighted by this Light.

Through nature, the nightly twinklers in the wondrous blue overhead, the unfailing freshness of the green out of the brown under foot; through the never-ceasing wonders of these bodies of ours, so awesomely and skilfully made, and kept going; through that clear quiet inner voice that does speak in every human heart amidst all the noises of earth and of passion; through these the light is shining, noiselessly, softly, endlessly, by day and night.

It is the same identical light that John is telling us of here that so shines in upon every man, and always has. There is no light but His. His later name is Jesus. From the first, and everywhere still, it is the light that shines from Him that lights men. He was with the Father in the beginning. He acted for the Father in that creation week. He gave and sustained all life of every sort everywhere, and does, though only a third of us know His later, nearer, newer Name—Jesus.

But the light was obscured, terribly beclouded and bedimmed, hindered by earth-fogs, and swampy clouds rising up, until we are apt to think there was no light, and is none; only darkness. Then He came closer, and yet closer. He came in nearer form so as to get the light closer, and let it shine through fog and cloud, for the sake of the befogged, beswamped crowd.

And then—ah! hold your heart still—then He let the Light-holder, the great human Lantern, be broken, utterly broken, that so the light might flash out through broken lantern in its sweet soft wondrous clearness into our blinded blinking eyes, and show us the real way back home. It was in that breaking that it got that wondrous exquisite red tingeing that becomes the unfailing hall-mark, the unmistakable evidence of the real thing of light.

And it's only as men know of this latest coming of the light, this tremendous tragic Jesus-coming of the light, that they can come into the full light. That's the reason He came in the way He did. That's the reason when He gets possession of us there's the passion to take the full Jesus-light out to every one. And this passion burns in us and through us, and ours, and sweeps all in the sweep of its tender holy flame. In this way every man may be fully lit, and so in following the Jesus-light he shall not walk in the darkness where he has been, but in the sweet clear light of life.

Looking for Recognition.

Then we come to the first of John's heart-breaking sentences. John had a hard time writing his Gospel. He was not simply writing a book. That might have been fairly easy for him with his personal knowledge and all the facts so familiar. But he is telling about his dearest Friend. And the telling makes his heart throb harder, and his eyes fill up, and the writing look dim to him, as he tries to put the words down.

Listen: He was in the world, and the world was made through Him, and the world recognized, or rather acknowledged, Him not. It was His world, His child, His creation. He had made it. But it failed to acknowledge Him. He came walking down the street of life. He met the world going the other way. And He gave it a warm good-morning greeting. And it knew Him full well. It knew who He was. But it turned its face aside and walked by with no return greeting. This is what John is saying. It recognized, it acknowledged Him not.

You mothers know the glad hour that comes in a mother's life when her little babe of the wee weeks knows her for the first time. She's busy bathing or nursing, or, she's just hovering over the precious morsel of humanity when there's really nothing needing to be done. And the babe's eyes catch her own and a smile comes, the first smile of recognition. And the mother-heart gives a glad leap. She murmurs to herself, "Oh, baby knows me!"

And when the father comes home that night she greets him with, "Baby knew me to-day." And there's a soft bell-like tender ring in her voice that vibrates on the strings of his heart. And all the folks within range are advised of the day's event. And the mother clear forgets all the sharp-cutting pain back there just a little before, in this joy, this look of recognition.

I knew of a woman. She was of an old family, of unusual native gift, and rare accomplishment. And her babe came. And the time came when ordinarily there would be that first sweet look of recognition, but—it didn't come. There was a defect; something not as it should be. And you mothers all know how she felt, yes, and you true fathers, too. She was heart-broken. And she turned aside from all the busy round of activity in which she had been the natural leader. And for years she devoted all her splendid talents, her strength and time, to just one thing, a very simple thing; only this,—getting a look of glad recognition out of two babe-eyes.

He looked into the face of His child, His world, for the look of recognition. But there was none. And He was heart-broken. And He devoted all His strength and time, Himself, for those human years to—what? One thing, just one thing, a very simple thing, only this: to getting a look of recognition out of the eyes of His child.

Aye, there's more yet here. He looks into our faces, eager for that simple direct answering look into His face and out of our eyes, yours and mine. And we give Him—things, church-membership, orthodox belief, intense activity, aggressive missionary propaganda, money in good measure, tireless, and then tired-out service—things! And all good things. But the thing, the direct look into His own face answering His own hungry searching look, that look in the face that reveals the inner heart that He waits for so often, and waits, a bit sore at heart.

For you know the eye is the face of the face. It's the doorway into the soul, out through which the soul, the man within, looks. I look at you, the man inside here looks out at you through my eye. And I look at the real you down through your eye. The real man is hidden away within, but looks out through the eye and is looked at only through the eye. We really give ourselves to Jesus in the look direct into His face which tells Him all, and through which He transforms us.

A Heart-breaking Verse.

Then comes John's second heart-breaking verse; but it is just a bit more heart-breaking in what it says. Listen: He came to His own home, and they that were His own kinsfolk received Him not into the house but kept Him standing out in the cold and storm of the wintry night.

One of you men goes home to-night. It's your own home, shaped on your own personality through the years. It's a bit late. You've had a long hard day. You're tired. It's stormy. The wind and the rain chill you as you turn the corner. And you pull your coat a bit snugger as you quicken your steps and think of home, warmth and comfort, loved ones, and rest for body and spirit, too.

As you come to the door you reach for your latch-key, and find, in the busy rush, you seem to have forgotten it, somehow. So you ring the bell or knock. And suppose—be patient with me a bit, please. Suppose your loved ones know you're there. You even see a hand drawing aside the edge of the window shade, and two eyes that you know so well peer out through the crack at you; then the shade goes to again. Yes, they know you're there. But the door, your own door, doesn't open. How would you feel?

And some one says to himself, "That's not a good illustration. That thing couldn't happen. It isn't natural." No: you're right. It isn't natural. It could not happen to you. I am sure it could not happen to me. If it could I'd be heart-broken. But this is what happened to Him! This is what John is saying here. He came to His own front door, and they whose very image revealed their close kinship to Him, received Him not into the home, but kept the door fast in His face.

Then there's a later translation. This old King James version bears the date of 1611, I think.

And the English Revision is dated 1881, I believe. And this American Standard Revision I am using has 1901 on its title page. But there's a later revision. It bears a yet later date, 1915, April 27. But it is a shifting date. Each translator fixed his own date.

This latest translation runs something like this: He comes to His own. That's you and myself. We belong to Him. He gave His breath to us in Eden. He gave His breath to you and me at our birth. He gave His blood for us on Calvary. We belong to Him. The image of His kinship is stamped upon us. We may not acknowledge it, but that can't change the fact.

He comes to His own, and His own—and here, as the scholars would say, there are variant readings. Let me give you one or two I have found. Here is one: He comes to His own, and His own—puts a chair outside the door on the top-step. It's a large armchair with a cushion in, perhaps. And then His own talks about Him through the crack of the door, or likelier, the window. It's reckoned safer to keep the door fast.

Listen to what he says: "He's a wonderful man this Jesus; great teacher, the greatest; the greatest man of the race; His philosophy, His moral standards are the ideals; wonderful life; great example." They fairly exhaust the language in talking about this Man. But notice. It seems a bit queer. The man they're talking about is outside the door. His own claim is left severely outside.

Some make it read like this: He comes to His own, and they who are His own open the door a crack, maybe a fairly respectably wide crack. We all like the word Saviour. Yes, we cling tenaciously to that. Selfishly, would you say? We want to be saved from a certain place we think of as down, that we've been taught about, and don't want to go to—if it's there; the way men talk about it to-day.

And we want to be saved into another certain place we think of as up, and where we surely want to go after we get through down on the earth, and must go away somewhere else; with that "after" and "must" carefully underscored. And we want to be saved from all the inconveniences possible along the way, and to secure all the advantages and help available: yes, yes, open the door a crack.

But be careful about the width of the opened crack. Let it be just the proper conventionalized width. Let there be no extremeism about the wideness of that opening. Things must be proper. For what would the other crack-open-door-owners think?

And then, too, yet more serious, this Jesus has a way, a most inconsiderate way of coming in as far as you let Him, and of taking things into His own hands. Certain people use that word "inconsiderate"—to themselves, in secret. Jesus changes some things when He is allowed all the way in. He might change your personal habits, your home arrangements, some of your social customs and your business plans.

Of course He changes only what needs changing, as He sees it. But—then—you—well, some things can be carried too far—to suit you. This Jesus has the all habit. He contracted it when He was down on the earth. Our needs grew the habit. He gave all. And He has a way of coming in all the way, and of reaching in His pierced hand and taking all.

He might even put His hand in on that most sacred thing, that holiest of all, that you guard most jealously—that box. It has heavy hinges, and double padlocks, and the keys are held hard under the thumb of your will. Of course there may really not be much in it; and again there may be very much. But much or little, it is securely kept under that thick broad thumb of yours.

Oh! you give; of course; yes, yes, we're all good proper Christian folk here. We give a tenth, and even much more. We support an aggressive missionary propaganda. That's the thing, you know, in our day, for good church people. We give to all the good things. Ye-es, no doubt. And we are very careful, too, that that inconsiderate Hand shall not disturb the greater bulk that remains between hinge and lock. That's yours. Of course you are His, redeemed, saved by His blood.

Well, well, how these pronouns, "His," "ours," do get mixed up! How lovely some things are to sing about, in church, and special services, at Keswick and Northfield. But through it all we hold hard to that key, we don't let go—even to Him, though it is He who entrusts all to our temporary keeping. We do guard the width of that opening crack, do we not?

One day I looked through that crack and caught a glimpse of His face looking through full in my own, with those eyes of His. And at first I wanted to take the door clear off of its hinges and stand it outside against the bricks, and leave the whole door-space wide for Him.

But I've learned better. No man wants to leave the doorway of his life unguarded. He must keep the strong hand of his controlling purpose on the knob of the front door of his life. There are others than He, evil ones, cunningly subtle ones, standing just at the corner watching for such an opportunity. And they step quickly slyly in under your untaught unsuspicious eyes, and get things badly tangled in your life. There's a better, a stronger way.

Here's the personal translation that I try now, by His help, to work out into living words, the language of life. He comes to His own, and His own opens the door wide, and holds it wide open, that He may come in all the way, and cleanse, and change, readjust, and then shape over on the shape of His own presence.

But every one must work out his own translation of that; and every one does. And the crowd reads—not this printed version. It reads this other translation, the one nearest, in such big print, the one our lives work out daily. That's the translation they prefer. And that's the translation they're being influenced by, and influenced by tremendously.

He Came to His Own.

In certain circles in England, they tell of a certain physician years ago. He came of a very humble family. His father was a gardener on a gentleman's estate. And the father died. And the mother wasn't able to pay her son's schooling. But a storekeeper in the village liked this little bright boy and sent him to school. And he went on through the higher schooling, became a physician, and began his practice in London. He became skilled, and then famous, and then wealthy.

He remembered his dear old mother, of course. He sent her money, and fabrics for dresses, and wrote her. But for a long time, in the busy absorption of his life, he had not been to see her. And the dear old mother in the little cottage in the country lived in the sweet consciousness that her son was a great physician up in the great London. He was her chief topic of conversation. When the neighbours were in she would always talk of her son, her Laddie, she called him.

"He's so good to me, my Laddie is. He sends me money. I put it in the bank. He sends me cloth for dresses; it's quite too good for a plain body like me. And he writes me letters, such good letters, wonderful letters. But he's so busy up there, that he hasn't been to see me for a long time now. You know he's a great doctor now, and he has great skill, and there are so many needing him. And he's no time at all, even for himself, I expect. But"—she would always finish her talk as they sat over the tea by saying, half to herself, really more to herself than to the little group, with a half-repressed longing sigh, "but, I wish, I just wish I could see my Laddie."

Then some changes took place on the estate. And the cottage where she had lived so long must be given up. And the dear old woman had to make new plans. And she cudgeled her old head, and thought, and at last she said to herself, "I know what I'll do. I'll go-up to London, and I'll live with Laddie. He'll be so glad to have me." And bright-coloured visions flitted through her mind, as she sat over her tea by the open grate. But she wouldn't send him word; no, no, she would surprise him, and add to his pleasure.

And the dear old soul, in her fine simplicity, did not think into what this would mean, nor of the difference that had grown up with the years, in manner of life, between her son and herself. He was a cultured gentleman, with his well-appointed city home, and the circle of friends that had grown up about him. And she was a simple uncultured country woman with a broad provincial twist on her tongue. But she was blissfully unconscious of this. She would go and live with her Laddie. It would be so delightful for them both.

And so she went. It was her first train journey, and quite a time of it she had finding the house. But at last she stands looking up at the house. "Ugh! does my Laddie live here! in this great mansion?" But there was the name on the door-plate. There was no mistaking that. And so she rang the bell. "Is the doctor in?" She could hardly get the word "doctor" out. She had never called him that before, just Laddie. But now she must say it. "Is the doctor in?" And the word almost stuck in her throat as she thought to herself, "This poor man opening the door doesn't know that the 'doctor' really belongs to me."

But in a hard voice the servant said that it was past the hours. She couldn't see the doctor.

"Ah! bat," she said, quite taken by surprise at being held there, "I must see him."

"But, I tell you, it's quite too late to see him to-day."

But she resolutely put her stout country-boot in the crack of the door, and her English jaw set in true English fashion, and she said with that quietness that has the subtle touch of danger in it, "I'll see the doctor."

And the servant looked puzzled and went to report about this strangely insistent woman. And the doctor was annoyed by the interruption in the midst of something that was absorbing him. He said sharply, "It's past the hours; I can see no one."

"I told her so, sir," replied the man deferentially, "but she insists in a strange way, sir."

"What's she like?"

"Oh, just a plain country body, sir."

"Well, show her up."

And I am glad to remember that she had a warm embrace of his strong arms, as he instantly recognized her in the doorway, while the servant stared. Then he said rather nervously as the servant discreetly withdrew, "How did you happen to come? Why didn't you send word? Has anything happened?" And then as she sat by the fire sipping a cup of tea, she told the story, in her own simple slow way, and ended up with, "And now I'm coming to live with you, Laddie." And the old eyes behind the spectacles beamed, and the dear old wrinkled face glowed.

And he poked the fire, and tried to think You know, our English friends depend almost wholly on the open grate fire, as we do so largely in the South. And it's a great thing, is the open grate fire. It's a fire. It warms your body, at least in front in extreme weather. But it's more than a fire. It's a stimulus to thought. It refreshes your spirit, and rests your tired nerves, and it is a wonderful thing to help you unravel knotty problems. So he poked the fire and thought, while she, quite unconscious of his embarrassment, went on sipping her tea and talking.

It would never do to have her come there, he thought. And his thoughts went to the circle of friends at the dinner table in the evening, and to the critical city servants that ran his bachelor establishment. And just then his ear caught anew the broad provincial twist on her tongue. He had never noticed it so broad, so decided, before. And she was talking the small countryside talk, chickens and an epidemic among them. And that grated strangely. It certainly wouldn't do to have her come there.

Then the tide began to rise gently on the beach of his heart. He thought, "She's my mother. And if mother wants to come here, here she comes." And he straightened up in his chair, as he gave a gentler touch to a blazing lump of coal. Then the tide ebbed. It began running out again. "No, it would hardly do." And he poked and thought. Finally he broke into her run of talk.

"Mother, you know it is not very healthful here. We have bad fogs in London. And you're used to the wholesome country air. It wouldn't agree with you here, I'm afraid. I'll get a little cottage on the edge of town, and I'll come and see you very often."

And the dear old woman sensed at once just what he was thinking. She was not stupid, if she was just a plain homely body. He got his brains from his simple country mother, as many a man of note has done. But she spoke not of what she felt. She simply said, with that quietness which grows out of strong self-control:

"It's a bit late the night, Laddie, I'm thinking, to be talking about new plans."

And he said softly, "Forgive me, mother: it is late, I forgot." And he showed her to her sleeping apartment.

"And where do you sleep, Laddie?"

"Right here, mother, this first door on the left. Be sure to call me if you need anything."

And he bade her a tender "good-night," and went back to his study to do some more thinking and planning. And very late he came up to his sleeping-chamber. And he was just cuddling his head into the soft pillow for the night, when the door opened, so softly, and in there came a little body in simple white night garb, with a quaint old-fashioned nightcap on, candle in hand. She came in very softly. And he started up.

"Mother, are you ill? What's the matter?"

And she came over very quietly, and put down the candle on the table before she answered.

And then softly:

"No, no, Laddie, I'm not ill. I just came to tuck you in for the night as I used to do at home. ... Lie still, my Laddie."

And she tucked the clothes about his neck, and smoothed his hair, and patted his cheek, and kissed his face. And she crooned over him as mother with little child. The years were quite forgot. She had her little son again. And she talked mother's love-talk to a child. "Good-night, Laddie ... good-night ... good-night ... mother's own boy." And a little more tucking and smoothing and patting and kissing, and then she turned so quietly, picked up the candle, and went out, closing the door so softly, her great strength revealed in her gentleness.

And he was just on the point of starting up and saying, "Mother, you must stay with me, right here"—no, the morning will do, he thought. But when the morning came she wasn't down for breakfast. And when he went to her room she wasn't there. It turned out afterwards that she had said to herself, "It doesn't suit my Laddie's plans to have me here. I don't understand why. It isn't his fault at all. It just doesn't suit. And I'll never be a trouble to my Laddie."

And so with that rare characteristic English trait of independence, she had quietly gone off early that morning before the house was astir. And he broken-hearted—I'm always glad to remember that—he searched through the wilderness of London for more than a year, searched diligently, but could find no trace of her. And then he was graciously permitted to minister to her last hours in a hospital where a street accident had sent her unconscious, and where he was chief of the medical staff.

She came to her own and her own received her not. He loved her, but it didn't suit his plans. He, Jesus, came to His own, and His own received Him not; it didn't suit their plans. Ah! listen yet further: He comes to His own, you and me, and His own—you finish it. Have we some plans, too, set plans, that we don't propose to change, even for—(softly) even for Him? Each of us is finishing that sentence, not in words so much if at all, in the words of our action. And the crowd reads our translation.

The Oldest Family.

"But," John goes on. That was a steadying "but." It was hard on John to recall how they treated his Friend and Master. But there is a "but." There's another aide, an offset to what he's been saying, a bright bit to offset the black bit. But as many as did receive Him. Some received. Jesus was rejected, yes, abominably, contemptibly rejected. But He was also accepted, gladly, joyously, wholeheartedly accepted, even though it came to mean pain and shame.

As many as received Him, John says, He received into His family. The conception of a family and of a home where the family lives, runs all through underneath here. They would not receive this Jesus because He didn't belong to the inner circle of the old families which they represented. They regarded themselves as the custodians of the exclusive aristocratic circles of Jerusalem. And Jerusalem was the upper circle of Israel.

And every one knew that Israel was the chiefest, the one uppermost nation, of the earth, with none near enough to be classed second. They were the favourites of God, all the rest were "dogs of Gentiles," outsiders, not to be mentioned in the same breath. To these national leaders of

Jesus' day, this was the very breath of their life.

"And this Jesus!" They spat on the ground to relieve the intensity of their contempt. "Who was He? A peasant! a Galilean! Nazareth!" Nazareth was put in as a sort of superlative degree of contempt. Of course, they could easily have found out about the lineage of Jesus. In the best meaning of the word, Jesus was an aristocrat. Apart from its philological derivation that word means one who traces his lineage back through a worthy line for a long way, and so one who has the noble traits of such lineage. In the best meaning of the word Jesus was an aristocrat. His line traced back without slip or break to the great house of David, and that meant clear back to Adam. The records were all there, carefully preserved, indisputable. They could easily have found this out.

I recall talking one day in London with a gentle lady of an old, titled Scottish family, an earnest Christian, trained in the Latin Church. In the course of the conversation she remarked, "Of course, Jesus was a peasant." And I replied as gently as I could so as not to seem to be arguing, "Of course, He was not a peasant. He chose to live as a peasant, for a great strong purpose. But He was an aristocrat in blood. His family line traced directly back through the noblest families clear to the beginning. No one living had a longer unbroken lineage. And that is the very essence of aristocracy."

In some circles, they count much, or most, on old families. In certain cities of our own country, east and south, this is reckoned as the hall-mark of highest distinction. When one goes across the water to England and the Continent, he finds the old families of America are rather young affairs. And as he pushes on into the East, some of the old families of Europe sometimes seem fairly recent. I remember in the Orient running across a family where the father had been a Shinto priest, father and son successively, through forty-five generations; and another where the father of the family has been successively a court-musician for thirty-eight generations. I thought maybe I had run into some really old families at last.

I come of a rather old family myself. It runs clear back without break or slip to Adam in Eden. I've not bothered much with tracing it, for there are some pretty plain evidences of ugly stains on the family escutcheon, running all through, and repeatedly. And then even more than that I've become intensely interested in another family, an older family, the oldest family of all. Arrangements have been made whereby I have been taken into this oldest family of all with full rights and privileges. My claims to aristocracy are now of the very highest, with all the noble obligations that go with it. That's what John is talking of here. As many as received Him, He received into His family, the oldest family of all.

These people refused Jesus because He didn't belong to their set. In their utterly selfish prejudice and wilful ignorance, these leaders shut Him out from the circles they controlled. But with great graciousness He received into His circle any, of any circle, high or low, who would receive Him into their hearts. To as many as received Him into their hearts He opened the door into His own family. He gave them the technical right of becoming children of His Father.

Their part of the thing is put very simply in two ways. They believed. They were told, they listened and thought, they accepted as true, they risked what they counted most precious, they loved. So they believed. And so they received. The door opened, the inner door, the heart door. He went in. That settled things for them. When He graciously entered their hearts, the inner citadel of their lives, that settled their place in this oldest family of all.

How We Don't Get In, and How We Do.

It is of intensest interest in our day to have John go on to tell, in his own simple taking way, just how we get into this God-family. First of all, he tells us how we don't get in. Listen: "not of blood," that is, not by our natural generation; "nor of the will of the flesh," that is, not by anything we can do of ourselves, though this has a place, a distinctly secondary place; "nor of the will of man," that is, not by what somebody else can do for us, though this too has its place.

These are the three "nots"; the three ways we are not saved. And it becomes of intensest interest to notice that these are the very three ways that the crowd is emphasizing to-day, some this, others that, as the way of being saved. The three modern words we commonly use for these three "nots" of John are, family, culture, and influence.

Some of us seem to be fully expecting to walk into the presence of God, and to get all there is to be gotten there, because of the family we belong to. This is probably stronger in some of us than we are conscious of. It's a matter of blood with us, our blood, our natural generation. We take greatest pride in showing what blood it is that runs in our veins. We trace the line far back to those whose names are well known. And this sort of thing has overpowering influence in our human affairs down here.

His gracious majesty King George is King of England, because he is the child of Edward and Alexandra. His one and only claim to the English throne is that at the time of accession he was their oldest living son. But that won't figure a farthing's worth when he comes up to the hearthfire of God's family. And I think he understands this full well. I'm expecting to see him there; not as King of England, but as a brother.

It is not a matter of blood. It's a blessed thing to be well-born. It makes a tremendous difference to have the blood of an old noble family in one's veins, if it is good clean blood. But it'll never save us. Salvation is not by lineal descent, not by family line. It is "not of blood." John clears that ground.

Some of us put great stress on what we are in ourselves. This looms big with a great crowd scattered throughout the earth. We know so much. We have gotten it by dint of hard work. We can do some things so skilfully. We have worked into positions of great power among men. Our names are known. Sometimes they are spelled in large letters.

The broad word for this is culture, what we have gained and gotten by our effort, of that which is reckoned good, and which is good. Culture is one of the chief words in our language to-day. Whether spelled the English way or the German, it looms big. It is one of our modern tidbits. It is chewed on much, and pleases our palate greatly. And culture is good, if it is good culture.

But, have you noticed, that you have to have a thing before you can culture it? No amount of the choicest culture will get an apple out of a turnip, nor a Bartlett pear out of a potato, nor make a Chinese into an Englishman, nor an American into a Japanese. Culture can improve the stock, but it can't change it. It takes some other power than culture to change the kind. Here we have to be made of the same kind as they are up in the old family of God. There must be a change at the core. Then culture of that new stock is only good and blessed.

This is John's second "not." It seems rather radical. It completely undercuts so much of our present day notions. If John is right, some of us are wrong, radically, dangerously wrong. Yet John had a wonderful Teacher whom he lived with for a while. And after He had gone, John had another Teacher, unseen but very real, who guided, especially in the writing of the old Jesus-story. The whole presumption is in favour of John's way of it being wholly right. And if that makes us wrong, we would better be grateful to find it out now, while there's time to change. Being saved is not a matter of what we can do, of our culture, though this has its proper place.

And some of us put tremendous stress to-day on influence, what we can command from others, in furtherance of our desires. Influence is spelled in biggest type and printed in blackest ink. Whether in political matters at Washington or at London; in financial, whether Lombard Street or Wall Street; or in the all-important social matters, or even in the educational, the university world, the chief question is, "Whose influence can you get?" "What name can you quote?" "Whose backing have you?" Influence and culture are the twin gods to-day. The smoke of their incense goeth up continuously. Their places of worship are crowded, with bent knees and prostrate forms and reverential hush.

Have you noticed that Jesus hadn't enough influence with the officials of His day to keep from the cross? No: but He had enough power to break the official emblem of earth's greatest authority, the Roman seal on the Joseph tomb. Rather striking that; intensely significant for us moderns. Peter hadn't enough influence with the authorities to keep out of jail. Sounds rather disgraceful that, does it not? Aye, but he had enough power with God to open jail-doors and walk quietly out against the wish of those highest in authority.

Influence has its proper place. It's good, if it is. But we are not saved by it. We are not saved by what some one else can do for us; "not of the will of man." Your mother's prayers and your wife's, and the influence of their godly lives will have great weight. It's a great blessing to have them. They help enormously. But the thing itself that takes a man into the presence of God, saved and redeemed, is something immensely more than this, some action of his own that goes to the roots as none of these other things do.

One time a deputation waited on Lincoln to press a matter of public concern. But his keenly logical mind discerned flaws in their impassioned and carefully worked out arguments. He waited patiently till their case was complete. And then in that quiet way for which he was famous, he said, "How many legs would a sheep have if you called its tail a leg?" As he expected, they promptly answered "Five." "No," he said, "it wouldn't; it would have only four. Calling a tail a leg does not make it one." So a simple bit of his homely sense and accurate logic scattered their finely spun argument.

Calling either family or culture or influence the chief thing doesn't make it so. These are John's three tremendous "nots." They rather cut straight across the common current of thought and belief and conduct to-day. We may indeed be grateful if a single homely drop of black ink from John's pen put into the beautifully cloudy-grey solution of modern thought clears the liquid and makes a precipitate of sharply defined truth that any eye can plainly see.

This is how we won't be saved. This is how we don't get into the family of God. It is "not of blood, nor of the will of the flesh, nor of the will of man"; not through family connection, nor by what we can do of ourselves simply, nor by what we can get some of our fellows to do for us, simply.

"But of God," John says. It is by Someone else, outside of us, above us, reaching down from a higher level, and putting the germ of a new life within us, and lifting us up to His own level. He puts His hand through the open door of our will, what we do in opening up to Him, through "the will of the flesh." He walks along the pathway of the earnest desire of those who would help us up, "the will of man." But it is what He does that does the one thing that all depends upon. His is the decisive action, through our choosing and our friends' helping.

I said it isn't a matter of blood, of lineage. Yet it is. That statement must be modified. Family relationship is of necessity a matter of blood. That's the very blood of it. This is a matter of blood; but not our blood; His. There has to be a new strain of blood. Our blood is stained. It is at fault. It is impure. There's been a bad break far back there in the family record, a complete break. We were powerless either to purify the stock, or to get over that gap, even if we admitted the need.

There had to be a bridging of that gap. It had to be from the upper side. The other fell short. The gap was still there. There had to be a new strain of blood. This was, this is, the only way. We get into that old first family only by the Father of the family reaching over the break and putting in the new strain of blood, the germ of the family life, and so lifting us up to the new level. And Jesus was God doing just that.

Our Tented Neighbour.

Then John begins a new paragraph. He goes back to tell just how the thing was done. Listen: _the Word, this wondrous One, became a man, one of ourselves, and pitched His tent in close amongst our tents._ There's only a stretch of canvas between Him and any of us. He wanted to get close, close enough to help, yet never infringing upon the privacy of our tents, only coming in as He was invited. But He has remarkable ears. A whisper reaches Him at once. And He is out of His tent into ours to help at the faintest call. That was why He pitched His tent in amongst ours, to be one of ourselves, and to be at hand in our need.

And then a touch of awe creeps into John's spirit as he writes, and the light flashes out of his eye with the intensity of an old picture surging to the front of his imagination again. There was more than a tent here, more than a man. Out of the man, out through the tent doorway, and tent canvas, flashes a wondrous, soft, clear light, that transfigures canvas and tent and man. John's face glows as he writes, "and we beheld His glory."

I suppose he is thinking chiefly of that still night on white Hermon. This despised Man had called the inner three away from the crowd, in the dark of night, and had gently drawn aside the exquisite drapery of His humanity, and let some of the inner glory shine out before their eyes. So the way was lightened for them as their feet were turned with His down towards the dark valley of the cross. I suppose John is thinking chiefly of this.

But this is not all, I am very sure. There's more, even though this may have been most. Glory is the character of goodness. It is not something tacked on the outside. It is some native thing looking out from within. So much of what we think of as glory and splendour in scenes of magnificence is a something in the externals, the outer arrangements. Splendid garbing, brilliant colours, dazzling shining of lights, seats removed a distance apart and up, magnificent outer appointments,—these seem connected in our thought with an occasion and a scene being glorious.

But John is using the word in its simple true first meaning. Glory is something within shining out. It is the inner native light that goodness gives out. "We beheld His glory." I think John must have been thinking of Nazareth. Thirty out of thirty-three years were spent in homely Nazareth. Ten-elevenths of Jesus' life was spent in—living, simply living the true pure strong gentle life amid ordinary circumstances, homely surroundings. This was the greatest thing Jesus did short of dying. He lived. Next to Calvary where the glory shined out incomparably, it shined out most in Nazareth. He hallowed the common round of life by living an uncommon life there. This was a revealing of His glory. So He revealed the inner spirit of simple full obedience to His Father's plan for His earth-life.

If we would only rise to His level! The way up is down. We are likest Him when we live the true Jesus-life regardless of where it is lived, on the street, in the house, amidst the ideals—or lack of ideals—of those we touch closest. It was a wondrous glory John beheld. And the crowd—no wonder that crowd couldn't resist Jesus. They can't even yet, when He is lived.

Then John goes on quietly to explain about that glory, how it came. He says it was "glory as of an only begotten of a father." The common versions with which we are familiar, the old King James, the English and American revisions, all say "the," "the only begotten of the Father." I suppose the translators wanted to make it quite clear that Jesus was in an exceptional way the very Son of God. And so they don't translate quite as John put it. They try to help him out a little in making his meaning clear.

But you will notice that this old Book of God never needs any helping out in making the truth quite clear. When you can sift through versions and languages down to what is really being said, you find it said in the simplest strongest way possible.

Here John is saying, "glory as of an only begotten from a father." It is a family picture, so common in the East. Here in the West, the unit of society is the individual. The farther west you come the more pronounced this becomes, until here in our own land individualism seems at times to run to extremes. Custom in the East is the very reverse of this. There the unit of action is not the individual, but the family. The family controls the individual in everything. We Westerners think we can see where it runs to such extremes as to constitute one of the great hindrances to progress there.

In the East, if a young man is to be married, he has actually nothing to do with it, except to be present in proper garb when the time comes. The fact that he should now be married, the choice of his bride, the betrothal, the time, all arrangements and adjustments,—all this is done by the families. The two that we Westerners think of as the principals have nothing to do, except to acquiesce in the arrangements of their elders. It is strictly a family affair.

Even so all that belongs to the family, of wealth, fame, inheritance, distinction, vests distinctly in the head of the family, the father. He stands for the whole family. And so, too, all of this descends directly from the father at his death to his eldest son. In some parts the father retires at a certain age, either really or nominally, and all becomes vested technically in his eldest son. And if the son be an only begotten son, then literally all that is in the father comes into the son. All the fame, the inheritance, the traditions, the obligations, the wealth, in short all the glory of the father comes of itself, by common action of events, to the son.

Now this is what John is thinking of as he writes, "we beheld His glory, glory as of an only begotten of a father." That is to say, all there is in the Father is in Jesus. When you see Jesus, you are seeing the Father. The whole of God is in this Jesus. This is what John is saying here.

Grace and Truth Coupled.

And then John does a bit of exquisite packing of much in little. He tells the whole story of the character, the revealed glory, of Jesus in such a few simple words,—"full of grace and truth." Not grace without truth. That would be a sort of weakly, sickly sentimentalism. And not truth without grace. That would be a cold stern repellent insistence on certain high standards. But grace and truth coupled, intermingling.

Of course real grace and truth always are coupled. They tell the exquisite poise that is in everything God does. Truth is the back-bone of grace. Grace is the soft cushioning of flesh upon the bony framework of truth. It is the soft warm breath of life in truth. Truth is grace holding up the one only standard of purity and right and insisting upon it. And as we look we know within ourselves we never can reach it. Grace is truth reaching a strong warm hand down to where we are and helping us reach it.

With God these things are always coupled. We get them separated badly, or would I better say, imitations of them. There is a sort of thing we have called truth. It is not so common now as a generation or more ago. It is a sort of stern elevated preaching of righteousness, but with no warm feel of life to it. I can remember hearing preaching in my immature boy days that made me feel that the man and the thing must be right, but neither had any attraction for me. It was as though a man went fishing with a carefully-made properly-labelled metallic-bait at the end of a long stout cord, and said, as he dangled it in the sinful waters to the elusive fish, "Now, bite; or be damned."

It was never put so baldly, of course, in words. And I was only a child with immature childish imaginations. Yet that was the feeling about the thing the child got. But it's scarcely worth while talking of that now except to point the contrast; things have swung so far to the other extreme.

The current thing to-day is grace without truth, or what is supposed to be grace. It is a sort of man-made substitute. It's something like this. Here's a man in the gutter, the moral gutter. It may be the actual gutter. Or, there may be the outer trappings of refinement that easy wealth provides; or, the real refinement that culture and inheritance bring. But morally and in spirit, it's a gutter. The slime of sin and low passion, of selfishness and indulgence and self-ambition, oozes over everything in full sight. The man's in the gutter.

And along comes the modern philosopher of grace, so-called. He looks down compassionately, and says, "Poor fellow, I'm so sorry for you. Too bad you should have gotten down there. Let me help you a bit, my brother." So he puts some flowering plants down in the slime of the gutter, and he brushes the man's clothes a bit, and his hair, and sprinkles the latest-labelled cologne-water over him, and pats him on the shoulder, and says, "Now, you feel better, my man, don't you?" And the man sniffs the perfume, and is quite sure he does. But he is still in the gutter.

There seems to be an increasing amount of this sort of thing over in my neighbourhood. How is it in your corner of the planet? There's an intense stress on environment; that means the outside of things. Better sanitation, improved housing, purer milk supply, and segregation of vice which seems to mean putting some of the viler smelling slime of the gutter, the slimer slime, all over in one guttered section by itself. But there can be no health there. It's a change of location that is needed!

The wondrous Jesus-plan is different. It holds things in poise. Grace and truth. Truth is Jesus stretching His hand up high, up to the limit of arm's length, and saying, "Here is the standard, purity, righteousness, utter honesty of heart and rigid purity of motive and life. You must reach this standard. It can't be lowered by the half thickness of a paper-thin shaving. You must come to this standard. The standard never comes down to you."

And the man in the gutter says, "I'll never reach it." And he is right. He never will—of himself, alone. Yet that's truth, true truth. "A hopeless case" you say; "utter impractical idealizing! Case ruled out of court." Just wait, that's only half the case, and not the warm half either.

Grace is Jesus going down into the gutter, the gutterest gutter, and taking the man by his outstretching hand, and lifting him clean up out of the gutter, up, and up, till the man reaches the standard, and is never content till he does. That was a tremendous going down, and a yet more tremendous lifting up. Jesus broke His heart and lost His life in the going down.

But out from the broken heart came running the blood that proved both cleansing and a salve. And out of the grave of that lost life came a new life that proved an incentive, and a tremendous dynamic. The blood cleanseth the inside of the man in the gutter, and heals his sores, restores his sight and hearing and sensitiveness of touch. The new life put inside the man makes him rise up and walk determinedly out of the gutter to a new location. He is a new man, with a new inside, in a new location. That threefold cord is ahead of Solomon's—it can't be broken.

And, if you'll mark it keenly, a new _in_side includes a new _out_side. The thing that in religious talk is called conversion is a sociological factor that cannot be ignored by the thoughtful student. The drunkard goes down to the old-fashioned sort of mission where they insist on teaching that the blood of Jesus cleanseth from all sin, and that the Holy Spirit will make a new man of you, and burn the sin out.

And something happens to the drunkard. He kneels a drunkard, drunk; he rises a man, sober. He goes to the hole he calls home. And at once a change begins to work gradually out. He treats his wife and children differently. He works. They are fed better and clothed warmer. He gets a better house in a better neighbourhood. The new sociological factor is at work. It began inside; it revolutionizes the outside.

Settlement houses, better environment, improved outer conditions of every sort, are blessed, and only blessed, after the inside is fixed or in helping to get it fixed. If that isn't done, they are simply as a lovely bit of pink-coloured court-plaster skilfully adjusted over an ugly incurable ulcer. The man is befooled while the ulcer eats into his vitals.

It's only the blood-power of a Jesus, the Jesus, that can fix the inside. He cuts out the ulcer and puts in a new strain of blood. Then the inner includes the outer. And the most grateful of all is the man. This is the Jesus-plan, John says, "full of grace and truth."

Grace is named first. It comes first. That is a bit of the graciousness of it. That's love's exquisite diplomacy. We feel the grateful warmth of the sun in the winter's air, and are drawn by it. We smell the fragrance of the roses and come eagerly nearer. We hear the winsomeness of a gentle wooing voice a-calling, and instinctively answer to it. And then we find the sun's power to heal and cleanse and its insistence on burning up what can't stand its heat.

We find the inspiring, purifying uplift of the flowers, drawing us up the hillside to the top. We find the voice—the Man—gently but with unflinching unbending determination that never yields a hairbreadth, insisting on our coming clear up to the topmost level. That's a wondrous order of words, and coupling of helps, grace and truth.

And this is Jesus. This is John's simple tremendous picture. This Man comes down into our neighbourhood, on our earth. He sticks up His stretch of tent-canvas right next ours. He insists on being His own true self in the midst of the unlikeliest surroundings. The glow of His presence shines out over all the neighbourhood of human tents. There's a purity of air that stimulates. Men take deep breaths. There's a fragrance breathing subtly out from His tent that draws and delights. Men come a-running with childlike eagerness.

Grace Flooding.

And now as Jesus comes quietly down the river road where John's crowd is gathered, John the witness points his finger tensely out, and eagerly cries out: There He is! This is the man I've been telling you about! He that cometh after me in point of time is become first in relation to me in point of preeminence: for He was before me both in time and in preeminence.

And then John adds a tremendous bit. He had just been talking about Jesus being full of that great combination of grace and truth. Now his thought runs back to that. Listen: "Of His fullness have we all received."

There's another translation of this sentence that I have run across several times. It reads in this way: "Of His skimpiness have we all received." I never found that in common print; only in the larger print of men's lives. But in that printing it seems to have run into a large edition, with very wide circulation. Men don't read this old Book of God much; less than ever. They get their impression of God wholly from those who call themselves His followers.

They watch the procession go by. Here they come crippled diseased maimed weakened in body, piteously pathetically crutching along, singed and burned with the flames of the same low passion that the onlooking crowds know so well, struggling, limping, crutching along bodily and in every other way.

And that's a crowd with very keen logic, those onlookers. It judges God by those bearing His name, very properly. And it says more or less unconsciously,—"What a poor sort of God He must be those people have. No doubt He has a great job of management on His hands. There are so many of them to provide for. And apparently there can't be any abundance, certainly no overflow, no surplus. He has to piece it out the best He can to make it go as far as possible."

"I think maybe I needn't be in any hurry to join that crowd, at least till I have to, along towards the end of things here. There would only be one more to carry. He has such a crowd now. And the resources are pretty badly strained, judging by appearances." So the crowd talks. Poor God! How He is misrepresented by some walking translations. "Of His skimpiness—-!" Be careful. Don't take too much. Be grateful for the crumbs.

Please clean your spectacles, and readjust them carefully, and if you are afflicted with the small-print Bible that seems in such common use, get a reading-glass and look here at the proper translation. That crutching, leather-bound translation is grossly inaccurate, if it is in such big print, and in such wide circulation. Look here. Can you see the words? This is the only correct reading: "Of His fullness have all we received." Put that into the print of your life, for your own sake and for the crowd's sake, yes, and for God's sake, too, that the crowd may know the kind of a God God is.

And as if John had a suspicion about possible bad translations, he did a bit of underscoring. That word fullness is underscored in John's original copy. It's a heavy underscoring, in red. The underscoring is in three words he adds: "Grace for grace." That is, grace in place of grace. It's a sort of picture. Some grace has been received. And it is so wondrous that nothing seems so good. And the man is singing as he goes about his work.

Then comes a sudden soft inrushing of a flood of grace so great that it seems to displace all that was there. Oh! the man didn't know there was such grace as this. It seems as if he had never known grace before. And the work-song is hushed into a great stillness, though the wondrous rhythm of peace is greater than before.

And then before he quite knows how it happens in comes another soft subtle inrushing flood-tide of grace that seems to displace all again. Some temptation comes, some sore need, some tight corner. You look to Him; lean on Him; risk all on His response. He responds; and in comes the fresh inrush.

And then this sort of thing becomes a habit, God's habit of responding to your need, need of every sort. It becomes the commonplace, the blessed commonplace that can never be common. That's John's underscoring of the word "fullness." May the crowds whose elbows we jostle get this underscored translation, bound in shoe-leather, your shoe-leather.

Then in his eagerness to make us understand the thing really, John makes a contrast. "The law was given through Moses; grace and truth came through Jesus Christ." The law was a thing, given, through a man. Grace and truth was a man coming, the very embodiment in Himself of what the two words stand for.

The law, the old Mosaic law, was not a statement of the full message of God. That was given much earlier. It was given to all. It came directly. It was given first in Eden, in its flood; and then continuously to every man wherever he was. It was given within each man's own heart, and through the unfailing flooding light in nature above and below and all around. The tide of its coming has never ceased in volume nor in steadiness of flow; and does not cease. That tide came to flood in Jesus. And that flood has never known an ebb.

But men's eyes got badly affected. They didn't let the light in, either
clearly or fully. The light was there, but it was not getting in.
Something had to be done to help out those eyes. So the law was given.
It was merely a mirror to let a man see his face, what it was like.

Here's a mother calling to her little son, "Come here and let me wash your face." And he calls out, "It isn't dirty." "Yes, dear, it is very dirty, come at once." "Why, no, mother, it isn't dirty; you washed it this morning." And the child's tone blends a hurt surprise and a settled conviction that his mother is certainly wrong this time about the condition of his face.

And if the mother be of the thoughtful brooding kind, she says nothing, but gets a hand mirror, and holds it before the child's face. That will always get a child's attention. And the boy looks; he sees his dirty face reflected. The blank astonishment on his face can't be put into words. It tells the radical upsetting revolution in his thought on that subject. How could it have happened that his face got into that condition! And the washing process is yielded to at least; possibly even asked for.

That's what the law did and does. It showed man his face, his heart, his need. It brings upsetting revolutionary ideas regarding one's self. There it stops. That's its limit. Then the Man who in Himself is grace and truth does the rest.

The Spokesman of God.

Then John quietly, deftly draws the line around to the starting point in that first tremendous statement. He completes a circle perfect in its strength and beauty and simplicity, as every circle is. If we follow the order of the words somewhat as John wrote them down, we find the bit of truth coming in a very striking, as well as in a fresh way. "God no one has ever, at any time, seen."

That seems rather startling, does it not? What do these older pages say? Adam talked and walked and worked with God, and then was led to the gate of the garden. God appeared to Abraham, and gave him a never-to-be-forgotten lesson in star study. Moses spent nearly six weeks with Him, twice over, in the flaming mount, and carried the impress of His presence upon his face clear to Nebo's cloudy top.

The seventy elders "saw the God of Israel, and did eat and drink," the simple record runs. And young Isaiah that morning in the temple, and Ezekiel in the colony of exiles on the Chebar, and Daniel by the Tigris at the close of his three weeks' fast,—these all come quickly to mind. John's startling statement seems to contradict these flatly.

But push on. John has a way of clearing things up as you follow him through. Listen to him further: The only-begotten God who is in the bosom of the Father—He has always been the spokesman of God. Look into that sentence of John's a little. It seems quite clear, clear to the point of satisfying the most critical research, that John wrote down the words, "the only-begotten God." The contrast in his mind is not between "God," and the "only begotten Son." It is a contrast whose verbal terms fit with much nicer exactness than that. It is a contrast between "God" and the "only-begotten God."

There is only one such person whichever way unity. They tell the whole story hanging at the end of John's pen. This little bit commonly called the prologue is a gem of simplicity and compactness.

It is John's Gospel in miniature, even as John's Gospel is the whole Bible story in miniature. You can see the whole of the sun reflected in a single drop of water. You can see the whole of both Father and Son in the action of love in these simple opening lines of John's Gospel.

Have you ever been walking down a country road till, weary and thirsty, you stopped at an old farmhouse and refreshed yourself at the old-fashioned well, with its bucket and long sweep? And as you rested a bit by the well you wondered how deep it was. It didn't look deep at all. The water was near, and it was so clear and sweet and refreshing, and so easy to get at for a drink.

Is it deep? So you fish a rather long bit of string out of your pocket, and tie it to a bit of stone you find lying close by. And you let the stone down, and down, and down, till you are surprised to find that the well is deeper than your string is long.

Well, John's opening bit is just like that. It seems very simple, easily understood at first flush in the mere statements made. The water is near the top. You easily drink. And you are refreshed. But when you try to find out how deep it is, you are startled to find that it is clear over your head.

But it is never over your heart. It is too deep for you to grasp and understand. You never touch bottom. But it's never beyond heart-understanding. You can sense and feel and love. You can open the sluice-gates into your heart, and have the blessed flood-tide lift and lift and bear you aloft and along. You can love. And that is the whole story.

Was John an artist? Is he making a rare painting for us here? Is he studying perspective, shading and spacing, to an exquisite nicety that is revealed in the very way he puts words and sentences and paragraphs together? I do not know. And if any of you think the thing I am about to speak of is due to a mere mechanical chance of the pen, I'll not quarrel with you. Though I shall still have my own personal thought in the matter.

But will you notice this? John begins his prologue with a description of a wonderful personality. He ends it with another description of this same personality. Both descriptions are rare in beauty and boldness, in simplicity and brevity. And right midway between the two, at almost the exact middle line of the reading, at what is the artistic center, stands the word "came."

That word "came" gathers up into itself and tells out to you the whole story about this twice-described personality. "He came" John says. That's the whole thing. First the He fills your eye, and then what He did—came. And as you step off a bit for better perspective, and change your personal position this way and that to get the best light, you find the picture standing out before your awed eyes.

It is a Man coming down the road with face looking into yours. He is truly a man, every line of the picture makes that clear to you. But such a man as never was seen before, with the rarest blending of the kingly and the kindly in His bearing. The purest purity, the utmost graciousness, the highest ideals, the gentlest manner, nobility beyond what we have known, and kindliness past describing,—all these blend in the pose of His body and most of all in the look of His face. And He is in motion. He is walking, walking towards us, with hands outstretched.

This is John's picture of Jesus. He came to His own. He came because His own drew Him. Out from the bosom of His Father, into the womb of a virgin maid, and into the heart of a race He came. Out of the glory-blaze above into the gloom of the shadow, and the glare of false lights below, He came.

Out of the love of a Father's heart, the Only-begotten came, into contact with the hate that was the only-begotten of sin, that He might woo us men up, and up, and up, into the only-begotten life with the Father.

Jesus was God on a wooing errand to the earth.

III

The Lover Wooing

A Group of Pictures Illustrating How the Wooing Was Done, and How the Lover Was Received

—"The Hound of Heaven."

"O thou hope of Israel, the Saviour thereof in the time of trouble, why shouldst thou be as a sojourner in the land, and as a wayfaring man that spreadeth his tent for a night?"—Jeremiah xiv. 8.

He came unto his own home, and they who were his own kinsfolk received him not into the house, but left him standing outside in the cold and dark of the winter's night. But as many as did receive him he received into his home, and gave each a seat in the inner circle at the hearthfire of God.—John i. II, 12. Free translation.

III

The Lover Wooing
(John i. 19-xii. 50)
The Mother of all Love-Words.

Brooding is love at its tenderest and best It is love giving its best, and so bringing out the best possible in the one brooded over.

Look into the nest where the word itself was brooded. It is a warm something, warm in itself, not a borrowed warmth. The warmth is its chief trait. It is a soft tender unfailing cuddling warmth. It cuddles and coos, it glows and floods a gentle comforting stimulating warmth. And the best there is lying asleep within the thing so brooded over awakes.

It answers to that creative mothering warmth. It pushes out, against all obstacles, and comes shyly and winsomely, but steadily and strongly, out to the brooding warmth, growing as it comes and growing most as it comes into closest touch with the warm brooder.

Brooding is the mother of all love-words,—friendship, wooing, pitying, helping, mothering, fathering, witnessing, believing. It is the mother-word, from out whose warm womb all these others come, warm, too, and full of gentle strong life. Its mother quality is so strong that we are apt to think of it only in connection with actual mothers, mothers among animals and birds and of our human kind.

But this is only one meaning, really a surface meaning, though such a fine deep meaning in itself. Its real heart meaning lies much deeper. Brooding is the mother of all love. It is its warmth that draws out that fine feeling that makes and marks friendship. It is its tender warmth that draws out that finest degree of friendship which knits with unbreakable bonds two lives into one.

It reaches out most subtly to knit up again the ends that have ravelled out under the sore stress of life. It bends compassionately over those hurt in body, and hurt yet more in their spirit by the greedy rivalry of life, and nurses into newness of life the shivering shredded hurt parts. In the more familiar use of the word it fathers and mothers the newly minted morsels of precious humanity, coming into life with big wondering eyes.

And it warms into highest life that highest love that, through the process of hearing, assenting, trusting, risking, giving the heart's devotion, comes to know God as a tender Father, and Christ as a precious personal Saviour. Whether in close friend, or ardent lover, gracious philanthropist, devoted parent, or earnest witness, it is the same warm thing underneath, at its fine task—brooding.

We think of it most in the mother. For it comes to its highest human perfection there. The true thoughtful mother is first and chiefest a brooder. She broods in spirit till her child looks into her eyes, bearing the image, in face and mental impress and spirit, which the brooding months have given. She broods over the inarticulate days when the babe cannot tell the felt needs except to a brooding mother's keen insight.

She broods over the baby-talk days; over the struggling days when the child would tell its awakening thoughts out in words, but doesn't know how yet; over the wilful days which come so early when the first battles come that decide the whole future.

With a warmth of tenderness and patience, and a strength of gentle wise insistence, more than human, she broods. It takes the very strength of her life, far far more than in prenatal days. So there comes, slowly, but as she keeps true to the brooding spirit, surely, the strong gentle self-controlled life out of the warm womb of her brooding life. So comes the child's higher birth, so preparing the way for the yet higher.

Now all this is at its native best in God. There only does it reach finest fruitage. Some day we shall recognize the meaning of that modest but tremendous little sentence,—God is love. This warm brooding something that comes, gentle as the dawning light in the grey east, fragrant as the dew of the new morning, irresistible in its pervasive persuasive presence as the rays of the growing sun, giving to us warmth, and life, and drawing out from within us warmth and life and beauty and strength, all in its own image, this is the thing called love. This is the thing that God is. As we know it we are getting acquainted with Him.

And if a break comes, instantly love in its grief sets itself with warmth and renewed strength to the new harder brooding task. It gives itself out yet more, regardless of cost, until in place of the broken fragments there comes a finer sort of life out of the warm womb of love, brooding, redeeming, bringing-back-again love. This is God. This is Jesus. John shows us Jesus as a picture of the brooding God.

Five Pictures of Jesus.

There are five wondrous pictures of Jesus in these newer leaves of the old Book. Three of them hang on the walls of Paul's tent-weaving study-room. There's the Colossian picture, the Creator-Jesus, infinite in power, making all things above and below and around, and holding all things together.[7]

Close by it in wondrous contrast is seen the Philippian picture. It is the Man-Jesus, emptied of all the upper-glory native to Him, bowing down low and lower and lowest, till in the form of a slave He hangs on a cross.[8]

And in contrast yet more striking and startling, close by its side hangs the Ephesian picture. It is the Enthroned-Jesus, back again in the soft, blazing, blinding glory of the Father's presence, seated at His right hand, far above all rule and authority and power and dominion and every name that is named. And as you stand awed before this picture your eye is caught by the artist's remarque sketch at the bottom. It is a broken Roman seal, and an open tomb, and a bird with swelling throat singing joyously.[9]

Then there's John's later Patmos picture of the Present-Jesus, standing now down on the earth in the midst of His candle-holding Church, but seen only by opened eyes. There He is seen as a Man of Fire, ablaze with light, intently watching, with tender but omnipotent touch waiting, ever waiting; with a patience unknown except in Him, still waiting.[10]

But John's earlier Gospel picture is of the Brooding-Jesus. The word "brooding" here takes in its fine deep significance. Jesus is seen here as a brooding Lover, by the warmth of His wooing love drawing out the warmth of an answering love. This is peculiarly and distinctively the picture of John's Gospel. There is a Man walking towards you in these pages. Turn where you will there

He is, and always facing you, with a gentle eagerness in His face and in the bend-forward of His body.

There is always a warmth, a gentle radiating comforting drawing warmth in His presence. This is the thing you feel most, the warmth. But it isn't the only thing. There's the purity. There are ideals that seem out of reach in their great height. There's the insistence on these ideals, rigid stern absolutely unbending insistence. You see these. You can't help it. You feel them tremendously. They seem to leave you clear out of reckoning, they are so high up. But there's the warmth, drawing arousing wooing, irresistible.

You come to find that the warmth of that presence is as irresistible as the ideals and the insistence are unbending. And the warmth woos you. It warms you, till there come the intense admiration of the ideals, and then the eager reaching of the whole being up towards them.

This is John's picture of the brooding wooing Jesus. This is God, in human garb as He comes to us in John's pages. Jesus is God brooding over us to woo out of us the love and purity, the purity and love, that He woos into us by the touch of His own warm presence.

John's little book is put together as simply as his sentences. And as you take it up, it falls apart almost of itself, so simple and natural are its divisions. We had a look at the opening paragraphs of the Gospel, those eighteen brief verses that open the doorway into all the Gospel holds for us. There is given chiefly John's simple vivid tremendous picture of a Person, coming with swift long stride and outreached hands.

Now we turn to the second part of the book. It runs from the nineteenth verse of the opening chapter on through to the end of chapter twelve. It is devoted to the great winsome wooing of this great human Person. Here we see Him on His wooing errand. He woos individual men. He gives the personal touch. He devotes Himself to one person, now here, now there. His skill and tact in personal dealing are matchless. But this is not the chief wooing of these pages. It is the nation He is wooing. With rarest strategy and boldness and persistence He lays loving siege to the nation through its leaders. This is central and dominant in all His movements here. This is the second picture in the gallery of John's Gospel.

It is a good thing to run through these fourteen pages of John's Gospel several times; to run through rapidly, though not hurriedly; to run through them as a story until it stands out in your mind as one simple connected, story. And then it will help greatly, if you are so blest as to have some boy or girl near at hand to whom you can tell it as a story in simple child (not childish) talk.

Pack the whole into one story of ten minutes, or fifteen: the man of the story;[11] how He tried to win the people's hearts;[12] how towards the end He spent a long evening with those who loved Him;[13] how awfully He was treated by those who hated Him;[14] then how wondrously He surprised His friends;[15] and then the little bit at the end where He prepares breakfast and has a walk and talk on the seashore with a little group of those who loved Him most.[16]

Tell that to a boy or girl as a short story. Use sensible words, but not one that your little listener wouldn't at once understand. Pretty sharp discipline for the story-teller, especially if you stop to put in a simpler word when you've blundered into a big one. The child will be held by it But you will get the most yourself out of the telling.

Warp-Threads.

Now as you read the second part over, it gradually sifts itself into several incidents about which the story is woven. These incidents form the warp-threads of the narrative. Into this warp are woven, sometimes little connecting links, sometimes quarrelsome discussion, sometimes exquisite bits of Jesus' teaching, and sometimes John's comments. And as the story grows it reaches one climax after another, each increasing in intensity, until the intensest is reached.[17] And these incidents fall naturally into groups. There are three chief groups that seem to stand out as giving the bolder points of the outline, and then smaller groups or single incidents that lie in between.

It is very natural that the story begins with the accounts of the deputation that was sent from Jerusalem by the official leaders of the nation, down to the Jordan bottoms where John the witness was drawing such great crowds. John modestly answers their questions about himself, and then the next day with dramatic intensity points out the Man for whom the whole nation has been looking for so long.

The only response from deputation and officials is a most significant disappointing silence, a silence fully understood both by John[18] and by Jesus.[19] But five Galileans in the crowd listening to John's reply seek out, or are brought into personal questioning touch with, Jesus, and then yield Him unquestioning belief and personal devotion. And these five come, in after years, to be leaders known wherever Christ's name is known.[20] So there begins the sharp contrast running throughout these pages, between the two sides into which Jesus' presence divides the crowds.

Then John traces the simple way in which the faith of these five men ran its tiny but tough tenacious tendril-roots down into their very vitals. A simple neighbourhood wedding occasion up near the old Nazareth home drew Jesus thither with His kinsfolk and His new-made friends. And then He meets the need of the homely occasion by helping out the shortened supply of wine in such an unusual way as reveals His character. And the conviction takes great fresh hold upon these five men that they have made no mistake. This Man is all they had taken Him for, and He is immensely more than they had thought into at first.[21]

Then comes a little connecting link. After the Cana visit, Jesus runs into the near-by town of Capernaum with His kinsfolk and friends for a few days, a sort of continuation of the neighbourhood courtesies.[22]

And then at once John goes to the intensest, and the most significant incident of this whole section of the book. It is the drastic turning out, by Jesus, of the traders in the temple-area at Jerusalem. This touched at once the national leaders' most sensitive nerve, and touched it roughly. It never ceased aching. This turning of the temple-area into a common market-place, which so jarred on the holy atmosphere of the place, and on Jesus' fine spirit, this was by arrangement with these leaders, and yielded them large profit. Here was the sore spot.

With one deft stroke John lays bare the secret of the intense hatred of Jesus by these national leaders, with which these pages teem, and which came to its bursting head at the cross. Long after, when Jesus had died and been raised, these five leading disciples find a new strengthening of their faith in recalling words spoken at this time by Jesus.[23]

Growing naturally out of this Passover visit comes the Nicodemus incident. Many of the Passover crowds were caught by the power of Jesus shown in the miracles He did, but had not the seasoned thoughtful faith of these first disciples. But one man sifts himself out by his spirit of earnest inquiry. The sharp contrast that runs throughout these incidents stands out here. This man is of the inner upper cultured circle, that controlled national affairs, that sent that Jordan committee, and that had been so upset by the temple cleansing.

Yet not only Nicodemus' earnest search for truth, and the questions asked by him, but the fullness and fineness of spirit truth in Jesus' words to him reveal the true faith of this rare inquirer; and this is verified by his later actions.[24] Clearly Jesus found here an opened door. Here is the first of those exquisite bits of Jesus' teaching that mark John's Gospel.[25]

These four incidents make up the first group of, what I think of as, the three chief groups of incidents in this section of John. The group begins at the Jordan, and runs up into Galilee, but in its interest and its chief incident, centres in Jerusalem. The action begins with John the witness, and swings naturally to Jesus. The contrast in this group of incidents is intense. With the same evidence at hand, first contemptuous silence and loving allegiance, then the beginnings of bitterest hate and of tenderest personal love, grow up side by side.

Then there is a sort of swing-away-from-Jerusalem group that includes three incidents. After the rejection of John's witness to Jesus[26] by the nation's leaders, Jesus withdraws from Jerusalem to the country districts of Judea. There He takes up the sort of work John has been doing, so bearing His witness to John. John had drawn great crowds down to the Jordan and in the neighbourhood of its tributary streams.

Now Jesus helps in arousing and instructing these crowds. There are two men preaching instead of one, and Jesus has the greater crowds. This is used to make trouble. It stirs up gossipy disputings. It is made to look like a jealous rivalry between the two men. And this supposed rivalry and disputing about the various claims of the two men become the uppermost thing. It reflects the characteristic spirit of the leaders. John greatly renews his witness to Jesus with fresh emphasis and earnestness.[27]

But as Jesus sees that His presence is only being made a bone of contention He quietly slips away from Judea, turning north through Samaria towards Galilee. Then comes the great story of the visit to Sychar, with the exquisitely tactful winning of the sinful woman to a life of purity, and then using her as a messenger to her people. Imbedded in the story is another bit of Jesus' simple great teaching talk.[28]

Then comes a brief connecting link. Finding no acceptance in Judea, His own country, Jesus goes to Galilee, where visitors at the Jerusalem Feast of Passover had been spreading the news of His words and deeds, and so a gracious welcome now awaits Him.[29]

And here in Galilee He wins the believing love of a roman officer of noble birth, whose son is desperately ill. The father's faith passes through three stages, the belief that comes to ask for help, the deeper belief that rests upon Jesus' word to him and starts back home, and the yet deeper that gets confirmation of Jesus' word and power in the recovery of his son from the very time Jesus spoke the assuring word.[30]

These are the three incidents in this group away from the Jerusalem district. It is striking that this group away from Jerusalem stands in sharp contrast with that first group centering in Jerusalem. There is rejection by the nation's leaders running from contemptuous silence to the beginning of open opposition. Here with less evidence there is acceptance by a Samaritan and a Roman; the one of no social standing; the other of the highest.

The rejection of Jesus by the leaders stands in contrast thus far with acceptance of Him by five Galileans, by a cultured scholarly aristocrat, a half-breed Samaritan, and a Roman of gentle birth. Acceptance seems to grow with the distance from Jerusalem. Yet everything hinged in Jerusalem. There had been the flood-light. Jerusalem was meant to be the gateway to the world. The irony of sin! The blinding of greed! The self-cheating of being self-centered!

Climbing towards the Climax.

And now, true to his controlling thought, John goes straight back to Jerusalem with his story, ignoring intervening events. There's another feast, not called a Passover, but commonly and probably correctly so reckoned, another crowd-gathering Passover. An extreme chronic case of bodily infirmity draws out the pity and power of Jesus, and the healed man takes his first walk after thirty-eight years.

But the thing is done on a Sabbath day, and gives rise to bitterest and murderous persecution, first on the score of Sabbath observance, and then because Jesus claimed God as "His own Father" in a distinctive sense. Friction fire may send out beautiful sparks. And the opposition brings out one of the choicest bits of Jesus' teaching to be found in John. This incident stands by itself.[31]

And now John reaches over a whole year with only a sentence or two for connection, and comes again to a Passover. The Passover was the pivot of the Jewish year and of Jewish national life. This Passover is made notable by Jesus' absence from Jerusalem, the only Passover absence of His ministry. And the reason is the violence of the persecution by the national leaders.

There is the feeding of the hungry thousands with a handful of loaves and fish. Was this the real Passover celebration? The multitudes fed by Him who was the Lamb of God and the true Bread of life? while the technical observance was empty of life! It wouldn't be the only thing of the sort, in ancient times or modern.[32]

Jesus withdraws from the crowds who would like a bread-maker for a king, gets a bit of quiet alone with His Father on the mountainside, and then walks on the water in the storm to keep His appointment with the disciples. Then follows a long disputation and another fine bit of Jesus' teaching.[33] These two incidents make another distinct group, separated from the previous one by a year on the far side and six months on the hither side. And the contrast continues, between the acceptance by the Galilean crowds and the intensifying opposition by the chief group of Jerusalem leaders.

Then comes the second chief group of incidents. About six months later Jesus returns to Jerusalem for the autumn Feast of Tabernacles. He boldly teaches in the temple in the midst of much opposition, bitter discussion, and concerted official effort against Him.[34] The dramatic incident of the accused woman and the conscience-stricken leaders[35] is followed by a yet more bitter discussion and by the first passionate attempt at stoning.[36]

Then the incident of the man born blind but now blessedly given his sight leads to the bitterest opposition thus far, and the casting of the man out from all religious privileges; and is followed by the rare bit of sheepfold and shepherd teaching.[37] These four incidents make up the second great outstanding group of incidents, and mark the sharpest clash and crisis thus far.

A few months later at another Jerusalem feast called the Feast of the Dedication, comes a second hotly impulsive riotous attempt at stoning, and then an attempt to arrest, both foiled by the restraint of Jesus' mere presence and personal power.[38] And another connecting link traces His going away beyond the Jordan River, where the crowds gather to Him, and are won to warm personal belief.[39]

Another little gap of a few months passed over in silence, brings the narrative to the third and last chief group of incidents in this part of the book, and so leads immediately up to the great final events of the whole book.

The illness and death of Lazarus draws Jesus back to a suburb of Jerusalem, Bethany. Then the stupendous incident of the raising of Lazarus leads to the official decision to put Jesus to death.[40] And a connecting link of verses tells of Jesus' cautious withdrawal, of the inquiring crowds coming to the approaching Passover, and of the public notice given that Jesus was under official condemnation.[41]

It is at the home feast given in Bethany as a tribute of love to Jesus that Judas, coldly criticizing a warm act of tender love, and gently rebuked by Jesus, gets into that bad heat of temper out of which came the foul bargaining and betrayal.[42] Another brief connecting link lets us see the crowds more eagerly inquiring for Jesus because of the raising of Lazarus, and the determined priests coolly plotting Lazarus' death, too.[43]

Then comes Jesus' faithful open offer of Himself in kingly fashion to the nation, with the tremendous enthusiasm of the multitudes, and the hardening of the official purpose to do the one thing that will offset this wild-fire enthusiasm.[44]

And then comes the apparently simple, but in meaning tremendous, incident of the inquiring Greeks. The Jew door is slamming shut, but the outside door is opening. Here the whole world opens its door, its front door, in these Greek representatives of the best culture the earth knew. But Jesus' vision never blurs. He understands; He alone. The only route to Greece and the whole outer world is the underground route, the way through Joseph's tomb.

And as the intense spirit-struggle passes, Jesus quietly goes on with His searching appealing talk to the crowd, and then slips away into hiding till His hour had full come.[45] And with breaking heart John sadly recalls Isaiah's wondrous foresight of just these days and events.[46] These are the four incidents in this third chief group.

And so the door shuts. The wooing ceases. This bit of John's story is done. The evidence is all in. The case is made up. The nation's door to its King shuts. The Lover's wooing of the nation ceases. John turns to a new chapter. No further evidence is brought forward. The case rests with the jury. The door had been shutting for a good while. The inside door-keepers had been pulling it hard. But the great Man outside had His hand on the knob delaying the shutting process, in the earnest hope that it yet might be quite stopped. Now His hand reluctantly loosens its hold. The knob is free. The inside pull does its work. The door goes to with a vigorous slam.

The wooing is not wholly done. There is still the indirect, the tacit wooing. There's still opportunity. All through that fateful night from Gethsemane's gate, to the last word at Pilate's seat the Lover is wooing. But it is wooing by action, by presence, by yielding. No pleading word is spoken. The direct wooing is done. Tender, earnest, insistent, patient, tremendous, irresistible in itself save to those who willed to resist anything and everything no matter what or whom,— wondrous wooing it has been. Now it's over. That chapter is done.

Way-marks in John's Narrative.

Out of this simple running account several things sift themselves, and stand out to our eyes. The action of the story swings chiefly about Jerusalem. The other parts seem but background to make Jerusalem stand out big. In this John's Gospel differs radically from the other three. They are absorbed chiefly with the tireless gracious Galilean ministry of Jesus, till the last great events force them to Jerusalem.

And the reason is plain. Jerusalem is Israel. It is the nation. Jesus is wooing the nation through its leaders. Why? For the nation's sake? for Israel's sake? Yes and no. Because these Jews were favourites of God? Distinctly no, though so highly favoured they had been in the wondrous mission entrusted to them. But because Israel was the gateway to a world Yes, for Israel's sake. Through this gateway, so carefully prepared when every other gate was closing, through this out to a world—this was the plan of action. And this will yet be found to be the plan. Through a Jewish gateway the King will one day go out to touch His world. This is the geography of John's story.

The action of the story swirls largely, too, about the great national feasts, the Passovers, the Tabernacles or harvest-home feast of the autumn, and one called "the Dedication," not elsewhere spoken of. To these came great crowds of pilgrim Jews from all quarters of the world, speaking many languages beside their national Hebrew, giving large business, especially to money-brokers and traders in the animals and birds used in the sacrifices. That classical Pentecost Chapter of Acts gives the wide range of countries and of languages represented by these pilgrim thousands. These feasts are the central occasions of John's story.

The time begins with John's preaching in the Jordan bottoms and reaches up practically to the evening of the betrayal. It is commonly reckoned three and a half years. That is, there are some months before that first Passover, and then the events run through and up to the fourth Passover, reckoning the unnamed feast of chapter five as a Passover. This is the chronology of John's Gospel. John's Gospel gives the only clue to the length of Jesus' ministry.

There are three groups of persons. There are the Jews. That is one of John's distinctive phrases. By it he means as a rule the official leaders of the nation, whom in common with the other writers he also designates by their party names, Pharisees, Scribes, Chief Priests, and so on. Among these the name of Caiaphas stands out, and later Annas.

Then there are the crowds, the masses of people that flock together in any new stirring movement. There are Galilean crowds, feast-time crowds including the great numbers of foreign pilgrim Jews, city crowds, and country crowds. They gather to John's preaching. They gather in great numbers in Jerusalem, and on the Galilean visits. They are easily impressionable, swayed by subtle crowd-contagion, stirred up and played upon cunningly by the opposition leaders.

They appeal greatly to Jesus, like unshepherded sheep. And the sick and needy ones, so numerous, draw out His pity and warm touch and healing power. They believe quickly, and almost as quickly are turned away and desert the cause they had so quickly and warmly rallied to. Fickle, unthoughtful, easily-swayed, needy crowds, but with the thoughtful ones and groups here and there who are really helped and who stick. These crowds are always in evidence.

And there are the disciples. There is the inner group of chosen ones who companion with Jesus, sharing His bread and bed, and close witnesses of His gracious spirit and unfailing power, with impulsive heady Peter and faithful steady John always nearest by. What a schooling all this was for them! And there are other disciples, not of this picked circle, but on most intimate personal terms with the Master, some of them, like thoughtful cautious Nicodemus, like the Bethany group of three, and Mary the Magdalene. And there is the larger, looser, changing body of disciples, mingling with the crowds, sometimes deserting, but no doubt with many thoughtful devoted ones among them. These are the leading persons figuring in John's story, grouped about the person of Jesus.

But these are simply interesting incidentals giving local colouring to John's story. We pass by them quickly now to a few things that take great hold of one's heart, that stand out biggest, and give the real action of life to the story.

Tapestry Threads.

As we unravel the fabric of John's Gospel there are three threads that stand out by reason of the distinctness of their colours. There's a thread of clear decided blue. There's a dark ugly black thread that gets blacker as it weaves itself farther in. And then there's a bright yellow glory-colour thread that shines with brighter lustre as the black gets blacker.

Trace the blue first, the thread of a simple glad acceptance of Jesus, and trust in Him. It deepens in its fine shading of blue as you follow it, true blue, the colour true hearts wear. From the very first Jesus is accepted by some, by many. And this continues steadily through to the very last. Some doors open at once to Him. Then under the influence of His presence and gentle resistless power they open wide, and then wider.

It is fascinating to trace the simply told story of growing faith, until one's own faith gets clearer and steadier and has more warm glow to it. To adapt Tennyson's fine lines, as knowledge grows from more to more there dwells in us more of the deep tender reverence of love, until all the powers of mind and spirit chord into one symphony of unending music. And the wheels of our common life move always to its rhythmic swing.

See how the crowds crowd to Jesus, and open up to the appeal of His words and acts and presence. Many of the pilgrim crowds of that first Passover believe, impressed by Jesus' spirit of helpfulness and His unusual power.[47] And the Galileans among them give Him warm welcome as He comes up into their country.[48] It is a great multitude that follows eagerly up on the east coast of the Galilean sea, hail Him as the long-expected prophet of their nation, talk of plans for making Him their King, and earnestly cry out, "Lord, evermore give us this (true) bread."[49]

Even in the midst of the bickering discussions at the Tabernacles Feast many of the multitude believed on Him, some as the long-talked-of prophet, some as the very Christ Himself.[50] And as He talks to His critics of His purpose always to please the Father, still others are drawn in heart to Him and believe.[51] And at this same time, as the criticism gets uglier, many make bold to speak out on His behalf[52] though it was getting to be a dangerous thing to do. As He feels compelled to withdraw from the tense atmosphere of Jerusalem, and goes away into the country districts beyond the Jordan the people come flocking to Him with open hearts.[53]

The Lazarus incident made inroads into the upper circles of Jerusalem, many of the influential social class with whom these dear Bethany friends seem on close terms, and who had been out there during those stirring days, believe on Jesus, and many of the common people, too, are won by that occurrence.[54] That tremendous raising of Lazarus had much to do with the great acclaim of the multitudes as Jesus rode into Jerusalem on the kingly colt.[55]

It is without doubt a sincere homage that these multitudes from far and near, and the home crowds, render, with their palm branches and garment-strewn roads, and spontaneous outburst of joyous song.[56] And now as John put his bit of a knotted summary on the end of this part of his story, he points out that even among the members of the Jewish Senate there were many real believers.[57]

But a crowd is a strange complex thing. It doesn't know itself. It's easily swept along to do as a crowd what would never be done by each one off by himself. And this works in good ways as well as in bad. Jesus drew the crowds and was drawn by them. He couldn't withstand the pull of the crowd. The lure of its intense need was irresistible to Him. Yet He knew crowds rarely.

He was never blinded by their enthusiasm. His keen insight saw under the surface, though it never held Him critically back from helping. He quickly notes that the belief of those first Passover crowds has not reached the dependable stage.[58] He is never held back from showing the red marks in the road to be trodden even though many of His disciples balk at going farther on such a road, and some turn away to an easier road,[59] so revealing an utter lack of the real thing. And even where there's real faith of the sincere sort it is yet sometimes not of the seasoned sort that can stand the storms.[60]

These crowds seem of close kin to more modern crowds. One touch of a crowd rubs out centuries of difference and shows one family blood in us all. Yet keep things poised. It was out of these crowds that there came the disciples and close friends to whom we now turn. There's gold in the crowds, finest twenty-four carat gold. It's all a matter of mining. Skilful mining gets out the gold. This wondrous Lover used the magnetic-current method of mining, the love-current. The strong warm current, the fine personal spirit current, drew out to Him the fine grains of gold in these human crowds.

Growing Faith.

Now we climb the hill where the disciples are. The crowds are in the bottom-lands. Many have started up the hill. Jesus always woos men uphill. You can always tell a man by where he is standing, bottom-land, hillside, higher-hill-slope, hilltop. We turn now from the crowds that believed to those whose personal acceptance of Jesus drew them into the inner circle.

The first three incidents trace the beginnings of faith in those first close disciples who came to be numbered among the picked inner twelve.[61] The first story is one of the rarest of John's many rare stories. It is characteristic of the real thing of faith that beginning with two they quickly number five. The attachment of the two to John, the Witness, reveals them as of the earnest inquiring sort, after the very best. John never forgot that talk with Jesus in the gathering twilight by the Jordan. It sends Andrew out for Peter, and John likely for James, while the Master gets Philip, and he in turn Nathaniel. That reveals the real stuff of faith. It has a mind whose questionings have been satisfied, a heart that catches fire, and feet that hasten out-of-doors for others. That's the real thing.

Their faith takes deeper root at Cana. A new personal experience of Jesus' power is a great deepener of faith, the great deepener. This is the only pathway from faith to a deeper realer sturdier faith. A man can get a deeper faith only by walking on his own feet where Jesus leads.

Their faith grows imperceptibly but by leaps and bounds. It grows down deeper and so up stronger and out farther by their companionship with Jesus through those brief packed years. What a school that was! the school of companionship with Jesus, with lessons daily, but the chiefest lesson the Teacher Himself. What a school it is! The only one for learning the real thing of faith: still open: pupils received at any time.

If we would shut our eyes and go with them as they company with Jesus through those wondrous days and events and experiences we may get some hold on how their faith grew. They actually saw the handful of loaves and fishes grow in their hands until thousands were fed. Their own eyes saw Jesus walking on the water.

It was out of their very hearts that they cry out through Peter's lips in answer to Jesus' pathetic pleading question and say, "To whom shall we go? Thou hast the words of eternal life."[62] And without doubt Thomas acts as spokesman for all when Jesus announced His intention of returning to the danger zone, and Thomas sturdily says, "Let us also go, that we may die with Him."[63]

But you are thinking of that terrible break of theirs on the betrayal night, are you? Well, perhaps if we call to mind with what an utter shock the events of that terrific twenty four hours came, intensified the more by the unexpectedness and the suddenness of it; and then if—perhaps—we may call to mind the more recent behaviour of some modern disciples who have had enormous advantages over them in regard to that terrific experience it may chasten our feelings a bit and soften the edge of our thought about them.

But dear faithful John never faltered. We must always love him for that. How humiliating for us if not even one had stood that test. And how their after-contact with John must have affected the others. John pulled the others back and up. And how their faith so sorely chastened and tested came to its fine seasoned strength afterwards.

These very events of the early days now come back with new meaning to them. Jesus' words at the temple cleansing, and the kingly entry into Jerusalem, shine now in a new light and give new strength to their faith.[64] But John himself brings us back to this again in that long talk of the betrayal night. So we leave it now. But blue is a good colour for the eyes. It reveals great beauty in the bit of tapestry-pattern John is weaving for us to trace these true blue threadings.

But there's more here, much more, that adds greatly to the pattern. There are faithful disciples and precious intimate friendships outside the circle of these future leaders. Take only a moment for these as we push on.

There's that night visitor of the early Jerusalem days. Aristocrat, ruler, scholar, with all the supercautiousness that these qualities always grain in, Nicodemus actually left the inner circle of temple-rulers who were as sore to the touch as a boil over John's drastic cleansing, and comes for a personal interview. His utter sincerity is shown in the temper of his remarks and questions, and shown yet more in the openness of Jesus' spirit in talking with him. For this is a trait in Jesus' dealings,—openness when He finds an opening door. It must be so, then and now. He can open up only where there is an opening up to Him. Openness warms and loosens. The reverse chills and locks up.[65]

It is in another just such situation but far more acute, that this man speaks out for Jesus in an official meeting of these same rulers. Timidly? have you thought, cautiously? Yet he spoke out when no one else did, though others there believed in Jesus. A really rare courage it was that told of a growing faith.[66] And the personal devotion side of his faith, evidence again of the real thing, stands out to our eyes as we see him bring the unusual gift of very costly ointments for the precious body of his personal friend.[67] It's a winsome story, this of Nicodemus. May there be many a modern duplicate of it.

In utter social contrast stands the next bit of this sort following so hard that the contrast strikes you at once. It's a half-breed Samaritan this time, and a woman, and an openly bad life. The Samaritans were hated by Jew and Gentile alike as belonging to neither, ground between the two opposing social national millstones. Womanhood was debased and held down in the way all too familiar always and everywhere. And a moral outcast ranks lowest in influence.

But true love discerns the possible lily in the black slime bulb at the pond's bottom and woos it into blossoming flower, till its purity and beauty greet our delighted eyes. Under the simple tact of love's true touch, out of such surroundings grows a faith, through the successive stages of gossipy curiosity, cynical remark, interest, eagerness, guilty self-consciousness that would avoid any such personal conversation, out and out comes a faith that means a changed life, and then earnest bringing of others till the whole village acclaims Jesus a Saviour, the Saviour.

And the very title they apply to Jesus reveals as by a flash-light the chief personal meaning the interview had for this outcast woman. In one way her faith meant more than Nicodemus', for it meant a radical change of outer life with her. And many a one stops short of that, though the real thing never does, and can't.[68]

Then the circle widens yet more, geographically. Jew, Samaritan, it is a Roman this time, one of the conquering nation under whose iron heel the nation writhes restlessly. He is of gentle birth and high official position. It is his sense of acute personal need that draws him to Jesus. The child of his love is slipping from his clinging but helpless grasp.

There's the loose sort of hearsay groping faith that turns to Jesus in desperation. Things can't be worse, and possibly there might be help. There's the very different faith that looks Jesus in the face and hears the simple word of assurance so quietly spoken. He actually heard the word spoken about his dying darling, "thy son liveth."

Then there is that wondrous new sort of faith whose sharper hooks of steel enter and take hold of your very being as you actually experience the power of Jesus in a way wholly new to you. As it came to his keenly awakened mind that the favourable turn had come at the very moment Jesus uttered those quiet words, and then as he looked into the changed face of his recovering child, he became a changed man. The faith in Jesus was a part of his being. The two could never be put asunder. So the Roman world brought its grateful tribute of acceptance to this great wooing brooding Lover. The wooing had won again.

And now there's another extreme social turnabout in the circle that feels the power of Jesus' wooing. We turned from Jerusalem aristocrat to Samaritan outcast; now it's from gentle Roman official to a beggaring pauper. It is at the Tabernacles' visit. Jesus, quietly masterfully passing out from the thick of the crowd that would stone Him, noticed a blind ragged beggar by the roadway. One of those speculative questions that are always pushing in, and that never help any one is asked: "Who's to blame here?"

With His characteristic intense practicality Jesus quietly pushes the speculative question aside with a broken sentence, a sentence broken by His action as He begins helping the man. In effect He says, "Neither this man nor his parents are immediately to blame; the thing goes farther back. But"—and He reaches down and begins to make the soft clay with His spittle—"the thing is to see the power of God at work to help." And the touch is given and the testing command to wash, and then eyes that see for the first time.

But the one thing that concerns us now in this great ninth chapter is the faith that was so warmly wooed up out of nothing to a thing of courageous action and personal devotion to Jesus. It is fairly fascinating to watch the man move from birth-blind hopelessness through clay-anointed surprise and wonder and Siloam-walking expectancy on to water-washing eyesight.

It is yet more fascinating to see his spirit move up in the language he uses, from "the man called Jesus," and the cautious but blunt "I don't know about His being a sinner, but I know I can see," on to the bolder "clearly not a sinner but a man in reverent touch with God Himself."

Then the yet bolder, "a man from God," brings the break with the dreaded authorities which branded him before all as an outcast and as a damned soul. And then the earnest reverent cry "Who is He, Lord, that I may believe?" reveals the yearning purpose of his own heart. And then the great climax comes in the heart cry, "Lord, I believe, I believe Thee to be the very Son of God."

And the outcast of the rulers casts in his lot with Jesus and begins at once living the eternal quality of life which goes on endlessly. What a day for him from hopeless blindness of body and heart to eyesight that can see Jesus' face and know Him as his Saviour and Lord! Growth of faith clearly is not limited to the counting of hours. It waits only on one's walking out fully into all the light that comes, no matter where it may lead your steps.

The Bethany Height of Faith.

The Bethany story is one of the tenderest of all. It touches the heights. It's a hilltop story, both in its setting amidst the Bethany blue hills where it grew up, and in the height of faith it records. It has personal friendship and love of Jesus and implicit trust in Him as its starting point. And from this it reaches up to levels unknown before. Faith touches high water here. It rises to flood, a flood that sweeps mightily through the valleys of doubt and questionings all around about.

At the beginning there is faith in Jesus of the tender, personal sort. At the close there's faith that He will actually meet the need of your life and circumstance without limit. The highest faith is this: connecting Jesus' power and love with the actual need of your life. Abraham believed God with full sincerity that covenant-making night under the dark sky. But he didn't connect his faith in God with his need and danger among the Philistines.[69] Peter believed in Jesus fully but his faith and his action failed to connect when the sore test came that Gethsemane night.

The Bethany pitch of faith makes connections. It ties our God and our need and our action into one knot. This is the pith of this whole story. Jesus' one effort in His tactful patient wooing is to get Martha up to the point of ordering that stone aside. He got her faith into touch with the gravestone of her sore need. Her faith and her action connected. That told her expectancy. Creeds are best understood when they're acted. Moving the stone was her confession of faith. Not that Jesus was the Son of God. That was settled long before.

No: it meant this—that the Son of God was now actually going to act as Son of God to meet her need. Under His touch her dead brother was going to live. The deadness that broke her heart would give way under Jesus' touch. The Bethany faith doesn't believe that God can do what you need, merely. It believes that He will do it And so the stone's taken away that He may do it. God has our active consent. Are we up on the Bethany level? Has God our active consent to do all He would? Is our faith being lived, acted out?

And the feast of grateful tribute that followed has an exquisite added touch. The faith that lets God into one's life to meet its needs gets clearer eyesight. Acted faith affects the spirit vision. There is a spirit sensitiveness that recognizes God and discerns how things will turn out.

Notice Jesus' words about Mary's act of anointing. There is a singularly significant phrase in it. "Let her keep it against (or in view of) the day of My burying." "Keep it" is the striking phrase. What does that mean? We speak of keeping a day, as Christmas, meaning to hallow the memories for which it stands. "Keep it" here seems to mean that. Let her keep a memorial. Yet it would be a memorial in advance of the event remembered and hallowed.

It seems to suggest that Mary thus discerned the outcome for Jesus of the coming crisis, and more, its great significance. The disciples expected Jesus' power to overcome all opposition. She alone sensed what was coming, His death and its tremendous spirit-meaning. And it is possible that the raising of her brother helped her to sense ahead another raising. For there is no mention of her at the tomb, as would otherwise have been most natural.

Her simple love-lit faith could see, and could see beyond to the final outcome. This is the story of the Bethany faith, faith at flood. This highest simplest truest faith, that had come in answer to

Jesus' patient persistent wooing for it, opens the way for the greatest use of His power on record.

There's one story more in this true-blue faith list. It is the story of the Greeks. At first it seems not to belong in here. There is no mention made of the faith of these men nor of their acceptance of Jesus. But the more you think into it the more it seems that here is its true place, and that this is why John brings it in, not simply to show how the outside world was reaching for Jesus, but to show the inner spirit of these men towards Jesus.

Whether the term Greeks is used in the looser sense for the Greek-speaking Jews,[70] or for non-Jewish foreigners, or, as I think most likely, in the meaning of men of Grecian blood, residents of Greece, the significance is practically the same, it was the outer world coming to Jesus. These had come a long journey to do homage to the true God at Jerusalem. Their presence reveals their spirit.

They were eye and ear-witnesses of the stirring events of those last days in Jerusalem. The stupendous story of the raising of the man out in the Bethany suburb was the talk of the city. And then there was that intense scene of the kingly entry into the city amid the acclaiming multitudes. They knew of the official opposition, and the public proclamation against Jesus. They breathed the Jerusalem air. That put them in touch with the whole situation.

Now notice keenly they seek a personal interview with Jesus. This is the practical outcome of the situation to them. It reminds one of that other man, under similar conditions though less intense, at an earlier stage, cautiously seeking a night interview. Their desire tells not curiosity but earnestness, and the very earnestness reveals both purpose and attitude towards Jesus.

And this is made the plainer by the very words they use as they seek out the likeliest man of the Master's inner circle to secure the coveted interview. They say, "Sir, we would see Jesus." The whole story of conviction, of earnestness, of decision, is in that tremendous little word "would." It was their will, their deliberate choice, to come into personal relations with this Man of whom they were hearing so much.

And it seems like a direct allusion to that tremendous word, and an answer to it, when Jesus, in effect, in meaning, says, "if any man would follow Me." Both the coming under such circumstances, and the form of the request, seem to tell the attitude of these men towards Jesus and their personal purpose regarding Him. It would be altogether likely that they accompany Philip as he seeks out Andrew. It would be the natural thing. And so they are with Philip and Andrew as they come to tell Jesus.

Then this would be the setting of these memorable intense words that Jesus now utters.[71] He senses at once the request and the earnest purpose of these men seeking Him out. It is for them especially that these words are spoken. And if, as some thoughtful scholars think, Jesus spake here, not in His native Aramaic, but in the Greek tongue, it gives colouring to the supposition. The intense earnestness of His words, and the revealing of the intense struggle within His spirit as He breathes out the simple prayer,—all this is a tacit recognition of the spirit of these Greeks.

The parallel is striking with the Nicodemus interview where no direct mention is made of the faith that later events showed was unquestionably there. It seems like another of those silences of John that are so full of meaning.[72] And the silence seems, as with Nicodemus, to mean the acquiescence of the inquirers in the message they hear.

This then would seem to be the reply to the request. They have indeed seen Jesus. And they accept it and Him, as most likely they linger through the Passover-days at hand and then turn their faces homeward. And so the warm wooing has drawn out this warm response from the cultured Greek world.

So we trace the blue thread in John's tapestry picture, the true faith that is drawn out from nothing to little and more and much and most, under the warmth of the brooded wooing of this great Lover.

The Ugly Thread in the Weaving.

Now for that ugly dark thread, the opposition to, the rejection of, the Lover's wooing. But we'll not linger here. We've been seeing so much of this thread as we traced the other and studied the whole. Ugly things stand out by reason of their very ugliness. This stands out in gloomy disturbing contrast with all the rest. A brief quick tracing will fully answer our present purpose. And then we can hasten on to the dominating figure in the pattern.

The opposition begins with silent rejection, moves by steady stages, growing ever intenser clear up to the murderous end. The sending of the committee to the Jordan to examine John and report on him was an official recognition of his power. The questions asked raise the possibility clearly being discussed of John being the promised prophet, or Elijah, or even the Christ Himself, and this is an expression of the national expectancy. The utter silence with which John's witness to Jesus is met is most striking.[73] Its significance is spoken of by both Jesus and John.[74]

The intensity of the resentment over the cleansing of the temple-area can be almost felt rising up out of the very page, in the critical questions and cynical comment of the Jews. One can easily see all the bitterness of their hate tracking its slimy footprints out of that cleansed courtyard.[75]

The cunning discussion among the great Jordan crowds about the purifying rite of baptism, stirred up so successfully by "a Jew," that is, probably by one of the Jerusalem leaders, would seem to be a studied attempt to discredit the two preachers, Jesus and John, and swing the crowds away. It was shrewdly done and might have dissipated the fine spiritual atmosphere by bitter strife and discussion had not Jesus quietly slipped away.[76]

This attitude of theirs is clearly recognized and felt by Jesus. He plainly points out that vulgarizing hurt of sin whereby God's own messenger is not recognized when He comes in the garb of a neighbour.[77]

Then things get more acute. The blessed healing of a thirty-eight-year-old infirmity leads to outspoken persecution, to a desire and purpose actually to kill Jesus. It grew intenser as Jesus' claim grew clearer. The issue was sharply drawn. He "called God His own Father, making Himself equal with God." They begin plotting His death.[78]

His prudent absence from Jerusalem at the time of the next Passover reveals graphically how tense the opposition had gotten. But even up by Galilee's shores they have messengers at work amongst the crowds exciting discussion and discontent and worse. In the discussion it is easy to pick out the two elements, the nagging critics and the earnest seekers. And the saddening result is seen in many disciples leaving Jesus and going back again to their old way.[79]

Then things got so intense that Jesus' habit of life was broken or changed. He could no longer frequent Judea as He had done, but kept pretty much to the northern province of Galilee. The settled plan to kill made His absence a matter of common prudence. This makes most striking His great courage in going up to Jerusalem at the autumn Feast of Tabernacles. He quietly arrived in the midst of much rumour and hot discussion about Himself, and begins teaching the crowds openly, to the great amazement of many.

At once begin the wordy critical attacks, egged on probably by the warmth with which many receive Jesus' teachings. There are three attempts to take Him by force, including an official attempt at arrest. But, strangely enough, the very officers sent to arrest are so impressed by Jesus' teaching that they return with their mission not done, to the intensest disgust and rage of their superiors.[80]

Early on the morning following there's a cunning coarse attempt to entrap Him into saying something that can be used against Him. A woman is brought accused of wrong-doing of the gravest sort, and His opinion is asked as to the proper punishment for so serious an offense. There's nothing more dramatic in Scripture than the withdrawal of these accusers, one by one, actually conscience-stricken in the presence of the few simple words of this wondrous Man.[81]

This is followed by the intensest give-and-take of discussion thus far, in which they give vent to their bitterest degree of vile language in calling Him "a Samaritan," and accusing Him of being possessed with "a demon." And then the terrible climax is reached in the enraged passionate attempt of stoning. It is the worst yet to which their fanatical rage has gone.[82]

Now they reach out to intimidate the multitude, by threatening to cut off from religious and civic privileges all who would confess belief in Jesus as Christ. And their spleen vents its rage on the man born blind but now so wondrously given sight of two sorts.[83]

The winter Feast of the Dedication a few months later finds Jesus back again in Jerusalem teaching. And again their enraged attempt at stoning, the second one, is restrained by a something in Him they can neither understand nor withstand.[84]

The Lazarus incident arouses their opposition to the highest pitch.[85] This is recognized as a crisis. Such power had never been seen or known. The inroads of belief are everywhere, in the upper social circles, among the old families, even in the Jewish Senate itself, notwithstanding the threatened excommunication. On every hand men are believing. Things are getting desperate for these leaders. They determine to use all the authority at hand arbitrarily and with a high hand. What strange blindness of stubborn self-will to such open evidence of power!

A special meeting of the Jewish Senate is held, not unlikely hastily summoned of those not infected with belief. And there it is officially determined to put Jesus to death, and serve public notice that any one knowing of His whereabouts must report their information to the authorities.

And as the incoming crowds thicken for the Passover, and the talk about Lazarus is on every tongue, it is determined to put Lazarus to death, too. This is the pitch things have risen to as John brings this part of his story to a close.

The Glory-Coloured Thread.

It is a relief to turn now to the chief figure in this tapestried picture of John's weaving. Here are glory-coloured threads of bright yellow. They easily stand out, thrown in relief both by the pleasing blues and the disturbing blacks. It is the figure of the Man on the errand, intent on His wooing, absorbed in His great task. Thia Man, His tremendous wooing, wins glad grateful ever-growing acceptance. And with rarest boldness and courage He persists in His wooing in spite of the terrific intensifying opposition.

The gentle softening dew persists in distilling even on the hardest stoniest soil. The gentle winsomeness of the wooing stands out appealingly as one goes through those fragments of teaching talks running throughout. The rare faithfulness of it to the nation and its leaders is thrown into bold relief by the very opposition that reveals their dire spiritual plight and their sore need.

The power of it is simply stupendous. As gentle in action as the falling dew it grows in intensity until neither the gates of death nor even the stubborn resistance of a human will can prevail against it. It is power sufficient to satisfy the most critical search, and to make acceptance not only possible with one's reasoning power in fullest exercise but the rational thing.

Look a bit at the power at work here. For in looking at the power we are getting a better look at the Man, and at the purpose that grips Him. Of the nineteen incidents in these twelve chapters fifteen give exhibitions of power. It is of two sorts, power over the human will, and miraculous power.

Eight incidents reveal power working upon the human will. In three of these—Nicodemus, the Samaritan woman, the accused sinful woman—the will becomes pliant and is radically changed, so morally affecting the whole life. In five—the temple cleansing, at the Tabernacles Feast, the first and second attempt at stoning, and the kingly entry into the city—the human will is stubbornly aggressively antagonistic to Jesus, but is absolutely restrained from what it is fully set upon doing.

In the other seven incidents the power is miraculous or supernatural. In three—turning the water into wine, multiplying food supplies, walking on the water—it is power in the realm of nature. In four—healing the Roman nobleman's son, the thirty-eight-year infirmity, giving sight to the man born blind, and the raising of Lazarus—it is power in the realm of the body, radically changing its conditions.

It will help to remember what those words miraculous and supernatural mean. Miraculous means something wonderful, that is, something filling us with wonder because it is so unusual. Supernatural means something above the usual natural order. The two words are commonly taken as having one meaning. Neither word means something contrary to nature, of course, but simply on a higher level than the ordinary workings of nature with which we are familiar. The action is in accord with some higher law in God's world which is brought into play and is seen to be superior to the familiar laws.

But the power, or the man that can call this higher law into action, is of a higher order. There is revealed an intimacy of acquaintance with these higher laws, and even more a power that can command and call them into action down in the sphere of our common ordinary life, until we stare in wonder. This is really the remarkable thing. Not supernatural action itself simply, tremendous as that is, but the man in such touch with higher power as to be able to call out the action, and to command it at will.

This is one of the things that marks Jesus off so strikingly from other holy men. There are miracles in the Old Testament and in the Book of Acts. But there's an abundance and a degree of power in Jesus' miracles outclassing all others. It is fascinating and awesome to watch the growth of power in these movements of Jesus. It is as though He woos more persistently in the very degree and variety of power that He uses so freely, and with such apparent ease.

Which calls out greater power, creating or healing? making water into wine or healing bodily ailment? Which is the greater, power in the realm of nature or the body? or in the realm of the human will? multiplying food or changing a human will? Which is greater, to induce a man voluntarily to change his course of action, or to restrain him (by moral power only, not by force) from doing something he is dead-set on doing?

This is the range through which Jesus' action runs in these fifteen incidents. Is there a growth in the power revealed? Is there an intenser plea to these men as the story goes on? Is there a steady piling up of evidence in the wooing of their hearts?

Well, creating is bringing into material being what didn't so exist before. Healing does something more. It creates new tissue, makes new or different adjustments and conditions, and it overcomes the opposite, the broken tissue, the diseased conditions, the weakness, the tendency towards decay and death. Clearly there's a greater task in healing, and a greater power at work, or more power, or power revealed more.

Then, too, of course, the human is above the physical. Man is higher than nature. He is the lord of creation. It is immensely more to affect a human will than to affect conditions in nature. The whole thing moves up to a measureless higher level. And clearly enough it is a less difficult task to enlighten and persuade one who seeks the light, and to woo up one who is simply carelessly indifferent, than it is to overcome and restrain a will that is dead-set against you and is bitterly set on an opposite course.

Of course, all of this is not commonly so recognized. It seems immensely more to heal the body than to change a man's course of action, or, at least, it appeals immensely more to the imagination. The man who can heal is magnified in our eyes above the other. The miraculous always seems the greater. It is more unusual. Stronger wills are influencing others daily. That's a commonplace. Bodily healing is rare. And all the world is ill. Things are ripe to have such power seize upon the imagination then and always.

And then, too, there are interlacings here of things we see and things we don't see. There is the element of the use of the human will in all miraculous action, whether in nature or among men. Behind both nature's forces and human forces are unseen spirit personalities, both evil and good. The real battle of our human life lies there in the spirit realm. Victory there means full victory in the realm of nature and of human lives. There is a devil with hosts of spirit attendants. The wilderness was a spirit-conflict of terrific intensity, ending in Jesus' unqualified victory.

Jesus' power was more than simply creative, or healing, or over human wills. It was the power of a pure, strong, surrendered will having the mastery over a giant, unsurrendered, God-defiant will. This underlies all else. But we've run off a bit. Come back to the simple story, and see how the power of Jesus is revealed more and more before their eyes. And in seeing the faithfulness and winsomeness of His power, see His wooing.

Intenser Wooing.

A look at the miraculous power first. The turning of the water into wine was simple creative power at work, creating in the liquid the added constituents that made it wine. The healing of the nobleman's son rises to a higher level. The power overcomes diseased weakened conditions and creates new life in the parts affected.

The healing of a thirty-eight year old infirmity rises yet higher in the scale of power seen at work. The Roman's child was an acute case; this an extreme chronic case of long standing. The acute case of illness may be most difficult and ticklish, demanding a quick masterful use of all the physician's knowledge and skill. The chronic case is yet more difficult eluding his best studied and prolonged and repeated effort. Clearly the power at work is accomplishing more; and so it is pleading more eloquently.

The feeding of the five thousand is creative power simply, like the water-wine case, but it moves up higher in the greater abundance of power shown, the increase of quantity created, and the far greater and intenser human need met and relieved.

The walking on the water was an overcoming one of nature's laws, a rising up superior to it. The universal law of gravitation would naturally have drawn His feet through the surface of the water and His whole body down. He overcomes this law, retaining His footing on the water as on land.

It was done in the night, but an Oriental community, like any country community, anywhere, is a bulletin-board for all that happens. No detail is omitted, and no one misses the news. And this like all these other incidents become the common property of the nation.

It is interesting to note in the language John uses[86] that the motive underneath the action was not to reveal power but simply to keep an appointment. But then Jesus never used His power to show that He had power, but only to meet the need of the hour. Yet each exhibition of power revealed indirectly, incidentally who He was.

There is an instance similar to this in the borrowed axe-head that swam in obedience to Elisha's touch of power to meet the need of the distressed theological student.[87] In each instance it is the same habit of nature that yields homage to a higher power at work.

But though there is here no increase of power shown yet the action itself was of the sort to appeal much more to the crowd. It has in it the dramatic. It would appear to the crowd a yet more wonderful thing than they had yet witnessed.

The giving of sight to the man born blind is distinctly a long step ahead of any healing power thus far related in John's story. There is here not only the chronic element, but the thing is distinctly in a class by itself, quite outclassing in the difficulty presented any case of mere chronic infirmity.

It was not a matter of restoring what disease had destroyed but of supplying what nature had failed to give in its usual course. It was a meeting of nature's lack through some slip in the adjustment of her action in connection with human action. There is not only the appealing dramatic element, as in the walking on the water, but the appealing sympathetic element in that this poor man's lifelong burden is removed.

And then the seventh and last of these, the actual raising of Lazarus up from the dead, is a climax of power in action nothing short of stupendous. Of the six recorded cases of the dead being raised this is easily the greatest in the power seen at work. In the other five, in the Elijah record,[88] the Elisha,[89] the Moabite's body at Elisha's grave,[90] Jairus' daughter,[91] and the widow's son at Nain,[92] there was no lapse of time involved.

Here four days of death had intervened, until it was quite certain beyond question that in that climate decomposition would be well advanced. Utter human impotence and impossibility was in its last degree. Man stands utterly powerless, utterly helpless in the presence of death. It is not the last degree of improbability. There is no improbability. It's an impossibility. The thing is in a class by itself, the hopeless class. And the four days give death its fullest opportunity. And death never fails in grim faithfulness to opportunity.

It is no wonder that all Jerusalem was so stirred. The common crowds of home people and pilgrims, the aristocratic families, the inner official circles, among all classes, this tremendous event won recognition of Jesus' power and claim, and with recognition personal faith. Nothing like this had ever happened. This is the superlative degree of miraculous power revealed in this matchless wooing of a faithless nation.

Love Wooing Yet More.

Now a look at the power at work in the realm of the human will, really a higher power, or power at work in a higher realm, though not commonly so recognized by the crowd. There are eight incidents here. And again we shall find the steady rise of the power seen at work. Three of these tell of the human will changed, and four of its being restrained against its will from doing that which it was dead-set on doing.

The ruler who withdrew from the midst of the disturbed temple managers for a night-call upon Jesus was radically changed in his convictions and his life-purpose. He had an open mind. The work was begun at that first Jerusalem Passover. Under the holy spell of John's presence he is drawn away from his enraged brother-rulers to seek the night talk. The frankness and fullness of Jesus' talk shows plainly how open he was and how much more he opened and yielded that evening. And the after protest in the official meeting of the rulers, and the loving care for the body of Jesus reveal how radical was the transformation wrought upon his will and heart by Jesus.[93]

The Samaritan woman is changed from utter indifference to a change of will and purpose that makes her an eager messenger to her people until they hail Jesus as the Saviour of the world. The change involved a radical face-about in habit and life amongst the very people who knew her past sinful life best. It meant more than change of conviction, that change actually put into practice across the grain of the habits of years, and of the lower passions, so hard to change. It is a distinct step up from the change in Nicodemus simply because there was so much more to change. The same power had more to do. And it did it.[94]

The story of the woman accused of the gravest offense is a double one in the power seen at work. She would naturally be hardened, and stony hard, shameless to the point of hopeless indifference in moral sense, and all this increased by their coarse publicity of her. And so little is said, but so much suggested of a change in her.

The purity of Jesus' face and presence would be a tremendous power of conviction. The gentleness of His quiet question would couple softening of heart with conviction of her sin. The word of counsel as she is dismissed would seem a mirror reflecting the inner longing of her heart and the new purpose stirring within, as memory recalls early days of virgin purity, and a wild hope within struggles towards life that there may yet be a change even for her.

The change in her accusers is, at least, as remarkable though wholly different. Morally hardened, as shameless and coarse as the woman as regards a fine moral sensibility; by their own tacit confession no better in practice than she in the point of morals raised; in their malignant cunning only concerned with the woman's sin as a means of venting their spleen upon the man they hated and feared,—what a hideous spirit-photograph!

Under the strange compelling power of Jesus' word and will, utterly conscience-stricken at being as guilty as she in the particular item under discussion, they turn, one by one, and slink softly out, until the last one is gone. As an instance of one will controlling and changing another will wholly against its will to the point of forcing out confession of personal guilt, it is most remarkable. One wonders if, under that tremendous conviction of personal sin, some of these were later included in those of the Sanhedrin who openly accepted Jesus. It is quite possible. It is not improbable.[95]

The fact is noted that the very language used here under the English indicates a different authorship of the incident than John's. Possibly a thoughtful delicacy of regard for the woman restrains John's pen if she were still living as he writes. And then later the Holy Spirit, who so tactfully restrains John's pen, guides another to fit the remarkable story in its place in the record.

The drastic turning of bargaining cattle-dealers and bickering money-brokers, out of the temple-area, and restoring it from a barn-yard to a place of holy worship, is a most remarkable illustration of restraint upon antagonistic wills at the point of their greatest concern. These leaders would gladly have turned Him out.

And who was He, this man with flashing eye and quiet stern word? A stranger, unknown, from the despised country district of Galilee. And they have authority, law-officers, everything of the sort on their side. Yet the restraint of His presence and will over them is as absolute as though they were in chains. They weakly ask for a sign and evidence of power. They themselves experienced the most tremendous exhibition of power the old temple-area had known for generations.[96]

The power of restraint at the Feast of Tabernacles is yet greater. Or it might be more accurate to say that it is a greater antagonism that is restrained by the same power. They are fully prepared now. The cleansing incident took them unawares. It made them gasp to think that any one would dare oppose them like that.

Now they are on guard. Then, too, their antagonism has intensified and embittered to the point of plotting His death. And they have grown more openly aggressive. There are three attempts at His arrest. Yet that strange noiseless power of restraint is upon them. They do not do as they would. Clearly they cannot. They are restrained. The man whose presence so aroused, also held them in check, apparently without thinking about it. His presence is a restraint.[97]

Then a second clash of wills comes a day or so later. Their opposition is yet intenser. There has been no cooling-off interval. His continued open teaching in face of their attempts at arrest puts fresh kindling on the fire. "No man took Him," but clearly they wanted to. Their open relations become more strained. He uses yet plainer speech in exposing their hypocrisies. This stirs them still more. Their hooked fingers reach passionately for the stones that would make a finish at once, and the green light flashes out of their enraged eyes. It's the sharpest clash yet. They are at a high fever point.

It seems to take a greater use of power to restrain. "He hid Himself" is the simple sentence used. This is one of four times that we are told of His overcoming the hostile attack of a crowd by simply passing through their midst and going on His way.[98] Perhaps something in the glance of that eye of His, or in the set of His face,[99] something in Him restrained them as He quietly passes through the uproarious crowd and goes on His way undisturbed. They are held back against their wills from doing the thing they are so intent on doing.[100]

A few months later He is back in Jerusalem. But the interval seems not to have cooled their passion, only to have heated and hardened their enmity. They at once begin an aggressive wordy attack. Then losing self-control in their rage they again reach down for the stones to kill Him at once. And again they are restrained from their passionate purpose, as Jesus quietly goes on talking with them. Again they attempt to seize His person. And the simple striking sentence used, "He went forth out of their hand," points to the extent of their purpose and to a yet greater use of His power of restraint over their unwilling wills.[101]

The last incident of this sort is the kingly entry into the city amid the enthusiasm of the pilgrim and city crowds. It says not a word about any attempt on their part nor of His restraint over them. But the very boldness of this wholly unexpected move on His part constituted a tremendous restraint. Their hate had gone through several stages of refined hardening during the few months preceding. The formal decision to kill, the edict of excommunication, the public notice that any information of His whereabouts must be made known, and the decision to kill Lazarus also,—all indicate the hotter burning of the flames of their rage.

Yet into just such a situation He quietly turns the head of His untamed unridden young colt of an ass and rides through the city surrounded by the crowds under the very eyes of these leaders and their hireling legal minions. The tenseness of the whole scene, the power of restraint so put forth, the volcano smouldering underfoot waiting the slightest extra jar to loose out its explosion, all are revealed in the little sentence so pregnant in its concealed dynamic meaning, Jesus "hid Himself from, them." There's an exquisite blending of restraint over them and boldness with cautious prudence. He was walking very close to the edge that time.[102]

So His power, shown so quietly but irresistibly before the eyes of all during those brief years, rises to a double climax nothing short of stupendous. Miraculous power in the realm of nature and of the human body had reached its climax in the raising of Lazarus, attested beyond question. Power over the human will both in affecting a voluntary change, and in actually restraining its action against its own set purpose, had risen to its climax in the bold open entry in broadest daylight into the capital where His death was officially and publicly decreed. The two climaxes touch. And it is tremendously significant that whereas they sometimes question His miraculous power, they could not deny His restraining power over themselves. How gladly they would if only they could.

And all this, mark you keenly, is a bit of His wooing. The wooing is ever the dominant thought in His heart. So He was revealing to them who He was. He claims to be the Son of God, their kingly Messiah. And He lived His claim. Power is the one universally recognized touchstone by which we judge God and man. His power told who He was even more than His tremendous words did. He was acting naturally. His presence among them thus natural, true to the power native in Him,—this was the wooing.

But there was more than power. There was love. There was a perfect blend of the two. With the power went the love. Nay, rather, with the love went the power. Love was the dominating thing. Jesus was love in shoes, God in action. Always there was the tenderness, the gentleness, the patience, the purity, the unflinching ideals, yes, the courage, the utter fearlessness tempered with a wise prudence. All these are the fuller spelling of love.

Always these went in closest touch with the resisted but resistless power. These are the two traits of God, two traits that are one. Men always think most of the power. God Himself always emphasizes most the love. But true power is simply love in action. The power is the outcome of love, and under the control of love.

This is the second of John's great impelling pictures. The first shows us the Person, the Man Jesus, God with us, God making a world, and then, in homely human garb walking amongst its people, one of themselves.

This second shows us the wooing. This Man, so tender in touch, so gentle in speech, so thoughtful in action, so pure in life, so unbending in ideals, so fearless in the thick of opposition, so faithful to the chosen faithless nation,—this Man Himself is the wooing. His words, His actions, His power, His persistence, His patience, this also is the wooing of this great God-Man-Lover. This is God spelling Himself out into human speech, wooing men out and up and in to Himself.

Jesus Recognised by all the Race.

And it is most striking to sit still and think into how this Lover was recognized by men of all nations, and how His wooing was understood and yielded to by men of all sorts. The intense Jew, the half-breed Samaritan, the aggressive Roman, the cultured refined Greek,—that was all the world. And all these recognized Him as some one kin to themselves, bound by closest spirit-ties, to whom they were drawn by the strong cords of His common kinship with themselves. The waves of His personal influence were, geographically, like His last commandment to His disciples. The movement was from Jerusalem to Judea, through Samaria, and out into the uttermost part of the earth and the innermost heart of the race.

And all sorts of men understood. Jesus wiped out social differences and distinctions in the crowds that gently jostled each other in His presence. The aristocrat and the cultured, the student and the gentle folk, mingled freely with simple country folk, the unlettered, the humblest and lowliest, all drawn alike to Him, and all unconscious of differences when under the holy spell of His presence. The wealthy like Joseph of Arimathea, and the beggar like the man born blind, the pure in heart like Mary of Bethany and the openly bad in life like the accused woman of Jerusalem,—all felt alike that this Jesus belonged to them, and they to Him.

The underneath tie of real kinship of heart rubbed out all outer distinctions. The old families of Jerusalem were glad to unlock their jealously guarded doors to Him. And the simple Capernaum fisherfolk were grateful when He shared bread and roof with them. All men recognized Jesus as belonging to themselves.

And the calendar has not changed this, neither Gregorian nor Old Style. Time finds the race the same always. Centuries climb slowly by, but the human heart is the same, and—so is Jesus. I was greatly struck with this in my errand among the nations. The East balks at the ways of the West sometimes. Many books say there is no point of contact between the two. The East balks at our Western organization, our rule of the clock, and our rush and hurry. Our Westernized church systems and our closely mortised logical theologies are sometimes a bit bewildering, not exactly comprehensible to their Orientalized mode of thought.

But they never balk at Jesus. When they are told of Him, and get some glimpse of Him, their eyes light, their faces glow, their hearts leap in response. You book people say there is no point of contact between Orient and Occident? But there is. Jesus is the point of contact. One real touch of Jesus makes all the world akin. No; that can be put better. One touch of Jesus reveals the kinship that is there between Him and men, and between all men.

In Japan it was the Portuguese that first took the Gospel a few hundred years ago. And you still find Japanese churches founded by the Portuguese. Fifty odd years ago it was the English tongue that again brought that message of life to them. But as I mingled among Japanese Christians of different communions and heard them pray, they were not praying in Portuguese nor in English. They had no thought that He was a Portuguese Saviour they prayed to, nor yet an English. They prayed in Japanese. They felt that Jesus spoke their tongue. He belonged to them. He and they understood each other.

As I listened to Manchu and Chinese, to Korean and Hawaiian pour out their hearts in prayer, I could feel the close personal burning touch of their spirits with Jesus. They and He were kin to each other. Their very voices told the certainty in their hearts on this point.

I recall a little old bent-over woman of seventy-odd years up in northern Sweden, a Laplander. She had come a long three days' journey on her snow-shoes to the meetings. Night after night as I talked through interpretation her deep-set black eyes glowed and glowed. But when one night an hour or more was spent in voluntary prayer she needed no interpreter. And as I listened I needed none. I felt that she knew that Jesus spoke Lappish. The two were face to-face in closest touch of spirit.

And so it is everywhere. The flaxen-haired Holland maid kneeling by her single cot knows that Jesus talks Dutch, and her homely hearthfire Dutch, too, at that. And the earnest Polish peasant in his Carpathian cabin bowed before the symbol his eyes have known from infancy is talking into an ear that knows both Polish accent and Polish heart. So with the German of the Saxon highlands, and of the simpler speech of the Teutonic lowlands. So with the olive-skinned Latin and the darker-hued African kneeling on opposite sides, north and south, of the great Central-earth Sea. Wherever knowledge of Jesus has been carried, He is recognized and claimed as their own regardless of national or social lines.

I knew a minister of our Southland, but whose public service took him to all parts of our country. He had been reared in the South and knew the coloured people by heart, and loved them. And when he returned to his Southern home town he would frequently preach for the coloured people. He was preaching to them one Sabbath with the simplicity and fervour for which he was noted.

At the close among others, one big black man grasped his hand hard as he thanked him for the preaching. And then with his great child-eyes big and aglow, he said, "Youse got a white skin, but youse got a black heart." And you know what he meant,—you have a black man's heart, you have a heart like mine. Your heart makes my heart burn.

Now Jesus had a Hack heart. He had a white heart. He had a yellow, a brown heart. He had a Jew heart, a Roman, a Greek, a Samaritan heart. Aye, He had a world heart, He had a human heart. And He has. There's a Man on the throne yonder, bone of our bone, heart of our heart, pain of our pain.

There's more of God since Jesus went back. Human experience has been taken up into the heart of God. Jesus belonged to us. And now belongs to us more than ever, and we to Him. The human heart has felt His tremendous wooing. It has recognized its Kinsman wherever He has been able to get to them, and it has gladly yielded to the plea of His love.

Jerusalem might carpenter a cross for Him, but the world would weave its heartfelt devotion into a crown of love for Him, bestudded with the dewy tears of its gratitude, sparkling like diamonds in the light of His face.

IV

Closer Wooing

An Evening with Opening Hearts: the Story of a Supper and a Walk in the Moonlight and the Shadows
—"The Hound of Heaven."
—Frederick William Faber.

IV

Closer Wooing
(Chapters xiii.-xvii.)
Knots.

The knot tied on the end of the thread holds the seam. The clinching of the nail on the underside holds all that has been done. Love ties knots to hold what has been gotten. The bit of prayer knots up the kindly act. The warm hand-grasp knots the timely word. The added word and act tie up all that's gone before. Hate imitates love the best it can. But its intense fires are never so hot.

The rest of John's book is simple. It is tying knots on the ends of threads. Five knots are tied on the ends of these same three threads we have been tracing.

There's a triple knot on the end of the blue thread of acceptance; an ugly tangled knotty knot on the end of that black thread of opposition and rejection; and a knot of wondrous beauty on the end of that yellow thread of winsome wooing. Chapters eighteen and nineteen tie two of these, the black and the glory-coloured.

Chapters thirteen through seventeen, is the first knot on the faith thread, the betrayal-night knot. Chapter twenty is the second, the Resurrection knot; chapter twenty-one the extra knot, the love-service knot. We take a look now at the patient skilful tying of the first knot on the end of that true-blue faith thread.

It's taken a good bit of careful work to get that thread, tearing loose, cleansing, spinning, twisting, careful handling, till at last a good thread is gotten, and is being woven into the warp. Now a knot is tied on its end to hold what has been gotten, and keep it from ravelling out, for there's a desperately hard place coming in the weaving.

There's a clean finish at the end of the twelfth chapter of John. There's a sharp break, an abrupt turn off to something quite different. The direct-wooing case is made up. There is no more added to it, except the indirect, the incidental. The evidence is all in. Wondrous wooing it has been, in its winsomeness, its faithfulness, its rare power. Now it is over. It's done, and well done. That door is shut, the national door.

Now another door opens. The inner door into Jesus' heart is being opened by Him. And the inner door into the disciples' heart is being knocked at that it, too, may open. It is the betrayal night. Jesus is alone with the inner circle. They have received Him. Now He will receive them into closer intimacy than yet before. They have opened their hearts to His love. Now He opens His heart to let out more the love that is there. Love accepted is free to reveal itself. And love revealing its warmth and tenderness and depth yet more calls out quickly a deeper, a tenderer love.

It's the Passover evening. They have met, the twelve and their Master, by appointment, in the home of one of Jesus' faithful unnamed friends. In a large upper room they are shut in, gathered about the supper board. As they eat Jesus is quietly but intently thinking. Four trains of thought pass through His mind side by side.[103] The Father had trusted all into His hands. He had come down from the Father on an errand and would return when the errand was done.

And now the hour was come. The turn in the road was reached, the sharp turn down leading to the sharp turn up and then back. It had seemed slow in coming, that hour.[104] Dreaded things seem to linger even while they hasten, dreaded longed-for things, dreaded in the experience of pain to be borne, eagerly longed for in the blessed result; as with an expectant mother. Now the hour's here.[105]

And yonder across the board sits the man so faithfully wooed, yet dead-set in his inner heart on a dark purpose, more evil in its outcome than he realizes. There must be more and tenderer wooing. He shall have yet another full opportunity. And under all is the heart-throb of love for these who are His own, being birthed into a new life by the giving of His very own life these months past. He loves His own, and will to the uttermost, the utterest, the mostest, limit of love and of time left Him before the great event. These are the thoughts passing quietly, clearly, intensely, through Jesus' mind as they sit at supper.

Teaching Three Things in One Action.

Now He acts.[106] Quietly He rises from the table, picks up a towel and fastens its end in His waistband for convenience in use, after the servant's usual fashion. Then He pours water into a basin and turning stoops over the feet of the disciple nearest Him. And before they can recover from their wide-eyed astonishment He begins bathing his feet and then carefully wiping them with the convenient towel. And so around the circle. Peter, of course, protests, and so calls out a little of the explanation. And then with tender passionateness he asks for the washing to take in all his extremities, head and hands as well as feet. How their hearts must have felt the touch upon their feet!

Then follows a bit of explanation.[107] But the chief thing had already been done. The acting was more than the speech. Three things the Master was doing. The teaching about humility lies on the surface, within easy reach. It was acted, then spoken; done, then said. It was sorely needed, and is. In it was the key to Jesus' great victory within the twenty-four hours following,[108] and would have been for them had they used it. Humility is the foundation of all strength and victory. Only the strong can stoop. It takes the strongest to stoop lowest. He who so stoops is revealing strength.

Humility is not thinking meanly of yourself; it is merely getting into correct personal relation with God, and so with men. It is our true normal attitude, as dependent creatures, as those who have sinned, as those who have been bought with blood. Everything we have is from Another, originally and continuously; we are utterly dependent. All rights have been forfeited by our wilful conduct; we retain nothing in our own right. And all we have now has been secured for us at the cost of blood; we are being carried at enormous expense. Not much room there for self-satisfaction, is there?

Humility is simply recognizing our utter dependence upon Another, and living it. And this controls our touch with our fellows. In this lies the secret of all strength,—mental keenness and vigour, sympathetic touch with others, and power of action in life and in service. All this touches the weakest spot in these men, and in—us.

But there's more here. The humility teaching is out on the surface. There's a bit under the surface, that they would soon be needing and needing badly. It's this: the thing in you that's wrong must be made right; and it can be. Every sin done by the man who is trusting Christ as his Saviour, every such sin must be cleansed away. And it can be. The feet-washing told this bit of tremendous truth.

These men trusted Christ. But their moral feet would get badly messed that night, mired and slimed by passionate betrayal and blasphemous denial and cowardly flight. The man going to the bath-house was clean on returning home except where his sandalled feet had gathered some soil from the road. These men were cleansed in heart through Christ. But the foot-soilings must be cleansed. These two things ring out. Sin must be reckoned with and cleansed out. And, blessed truth! it can be. This is the second bit. It would be brought to their remembrance that same night when the road they took dirtied them up so badly, and afterwards.

But there's a deeper, a tenderer bit yet here. There is the love touch. Jesus was giving them the tenderest touch yet of His love, to hold them. The personal touch is the tenderest. Man yearns for the personal touch, of presence, of lips, of hands. Something seems to go through the personal touch from heart to heart. The spirit-currents find their connection so. Jesus gave the tender personal touch that evening, the closest yet. His hands touched their feet, but He was not thinking most about their feet. He was reaching higher up. His hands reached past their feet for their hearts.

And they felt it so. Their hearts understood, if their heads didn't yet. Judas felt those hands reaching to touch his heart. And he had to set himself afresh to resist that touch. John felt it, and remained steady. Peter felt it and came back with flooded eyes. The fleeing nine felt that touch and yielded to it as they penitently returned. Love won. That personal touch did it.

But Jesus feels Judas' heart hardening as He touches his feet, and the gentle word already spoken availed not.[109] Now His great heart is sorely troubled for Judas.[110] He tries once again to reach his heart and stay his wayward feet. He reaches for his feet through his heart this time. They're all together about the table again. Quietly, but with tactful indirectness, Jesus lets Judas know that He knows. He says, "One of you is planning to betray Me."

The men stare one at another in questioning astonishment. Peter touches John's arm and with eye and word quietly asks him to find out. John reclining next to Jesus asks the question in undertone. And as quietly Jesus makes reply. Then the last appeal is made to Judas in the last delicate touch of special personal attention. Judas' unchanged spirit makes wordless answer. The hardening of the purpose is a further opening of a downward door and that door is quickly used by the evil one.

And Judas rises abruptly with jaw set and eye tense, and goes out into the blackest night the clouds ever shut in. So the first tremendous part of the evening's drama is now done. The wooing of Judas has been intense and tender clean up to the last moment, and resisted. Now that chapter is done. Another corner is passed. The extremes have—parted. One man has gone out. Eleven stay in, and in staying come closer.

Believe—Love—Obey.

The atmosphere clears now. That black cloud shifts. The pressure is relieved. The air changes. Breathing is easier. Jesus did His best to keep Judas in by trying to have him turn something— some one—out. But the something that held the some one is kept within, so the man goes out. That inside air was getting a bit thick for Judas. Love's tender pleading unyielded to makes breathing difficult.

Again Jesus begins talking in the cleared air. The hour had full come. The character of the Son of Man would now be revealed,[111] and in being revealed God's character would also be understood, and God Himself would show what He thought of Jesus by His personal recognition and acknowledgment of Him, and He would do it at once. The clock is striking the hour. Now He was going away. They would not understand.[112]

Then Jesus strikes the great key-note of their future conduct as He goes on. The thing is this: love one another. This is the badge He gives them to wear. It will always identify them as His very own. Peter picks up the one bit he understands, and is told that he cannot yet follow in the tremendous experience lying just ahead for Jesus, but some day he can, and will. And then to Peter's blundering self-confidence comes a plain tender reminder of his weakness.[113] So that wondrous fourteenth chapter that Christendom loves begins back in the thirteenth.

And Jesus goes quietly on as they still linger about the table.[114] He had been sorely troubled,[115] but He would have them not troubled by their doubtings regarding Himself. It is true that they were outcasts with Him, from their national home, but He would provide them a home, and a better one. They did believe in God. They should believe Him just as implicitly. This is the warp into which is woven the whole fabric of that evening's talk. The whole talk is a plea for their trusting loving acceptance of Himself as fully as of God. This word "believe" changes its outer shape three times during that evening, making four words in all, but it's always the same thing underneath.

So now the teaching goes on in freest exchange of question and answer. What a picture of how we may talk everything out with our Lord and get fully answered. Thomas' question helps Jesus to turn them away from thinking of a roadway of clay and sand to a Man. Philip's helps Him to insist on the presence of the Father in a distinctive sense within this Man so familiarly talking with them. And then four times over He rings out that word believe.

Then by a subtle turn He changes the word, though not the thing, to help them understand better: "If ye love Me."[116] That puts the thing at once up on the heart level. Believing is a thing of the heart. Their heads were bothered. He said in effect,—all your head questions will be answered in good time, but this thing is higher up than that. It's a matter of your heart. And so that word believe becomes love, its second shape. And with that is quickly coupled obey, the third outer shape He gives the word believe that night.

It is all the same thing underneath. Love is the heart side of believe, the inner side. Obey is the life-side of believe, the outer, the action side. The love looks out the window of the life and then comes out and walks down the street on an errand. Love doesn't simply love: it loves some one. Love that simply loves isn't love. Love comes to life only in the personal touch.

And love keeps in perfect rhythm of action with the one loved. That is the other way of saying obey. Obedience is the music of two wills acting together. Believe me, love me, obey me,—this is the three-noted music of the upper room; three notes but one music; a fourth note to be added later. This is the wondrous closer wooing.

"I go to the Father. We, the Father and I, will send the Holy Spirit to you. He will come in through this opened door of obedience. He will abide in you, come in to stay. He will be everything and do everything that you need in every sort of circumstance. Keep in closest touch with Him: this is to be your one rule. Your part is simple. Believe; that means love; that means obey."

So they talk around the table. Then there's thoughtful silence, which the Master breaks by saying, "Arise, let us go."

The Great Vine Picture.

Now they're walking down the street, silently, the Master in the lead, with John and Peter close by.[117] The moon is at the full. Now they see the temple, the moonlight falling full upon it. And the great brass grape-vine with which it had been beautified by Herod at his building of it shines with wondrous beauty in the enchantment of moonlight.

And now the Master is speaking again. Very quietly the words come as they still gaze at the beauty of the brass vine. Listen to Him, "I am the true vine, and My Father the vine-gardener." Here is the illustration that exactly pictures what He had been saying in the upper room. It supplies the fourth word, the fourth outer shape that word believe takes on, believe, that is—love, that is—obey, that is—abide.

Look at the vine, then you have the whole story pictured, simple, clear, full. Each of these four words grows out of the other as fruit out of blossom, and blossom out of the new branch and that out of the old stock of the vine: believe, love, obey, abide; vine, new branches, tiny blossom, fruit. The fruit grows out of the vine; yet it is the very life of the vine. Abide grows out of believe, yet it is the very heart and inner life of believe.

So He goes on ringing the changes back and forth, now here, now there. Pruning—that insures fruit, and more and better. Praying—that is the fruit, some of it; that naturally grows out of the abiding. "My words"—that is part of the abiding, the life-juice of the vine coming into branch and blossom and fruit. "Joy"—that is the rich red juice of the grape in your mouth. "Friends"—that is the other word for abide. That's what abiding makes and reveals. Abiding—that is what friends do: that's what friendship is, the real thing. Obey—that is the swing of step with our great Friend as we go along the road together. So these clusters of rich ripe fruit hang thick on the vine of this simple teaching-talk as they walk along in the moonlight.

And now they're passing through some of the narrower streets as they make their way east towards the city gate.[118] And these narrow streets are shadowed. And you feel the shadows creeping into His talk. The world will hate them. Of course. This is a natural result of the abiding. The outer crowd can no more put up with the Jesus-swayed man than with Jesus Himself. And the hate would be aggressive.

But if they would clearly understand ahead what to expect it would help them keep their feet when the worst storm came. And by staying steady and true through the worst that came, they would be of the greatest service. The Holy Spirit in them would reach out and talk to that outer crowd. He would make clear to them their awful sin in killing Jesus, the spotless purity and rightness of the absent Jesus, and the terrific fact that the prince of the world whom they rally to so faithfully is actually judged, doomed and damned. Then He adds, "now in a little bit I'll be gone from you. Then a little later, I'll be with you again."

So He goes on ringing the changes back and forth on this in simple conversational style. And now they are silent. The narrow street is quite shadowed. He lets them think a bit over His words. And the personal part takes hold most. And they talk softly together of what this means,—a little while and He is gone; again a little while, and He is back. They're plainly puzzled, yet restrained from breaking in upon His deep mood.

But with characteristic gentleness He speaks of what they would ask.[119] Clearly there is some terrible experience for Him and for them just at hand. But He reaches past to the joy beyond, as the mother forgets sharp pains in the joy of her new-born babe. And as He talks they think they understand now, but again He gently reminds of the storm about to break. And then He leaves them three wondrous words,—peace, good-cheer, overcome. In the midst of the worst storm there may be peace. In the thickest of tribulation the song of cheer may ring out. He has overcome. The outcome is settled. No doubts need nag. Sing! Sing louder! Christ is Victor!

This is the second bit of the evening's closer wooing, this long quiet talk about the supper table and along the road. It is wooing them up to more intelligence in their believing and loving. It's wooing them to trust Him, hold hard to Him, during the coming storm, when they wouldn't understand. Even when they can't understand, but stand in hopeless helpless bewilderment, they still can trust Him.

Taken into the Innermost Life.

They're outside the city-gate now, going down the path towards the Kidron Brook. Now comes the third bit of that evening's closer wooing.[120] And this is the tenderest, the most personal, the least resistible bit, the closest wooing of all. He takes them into His innermost heart-life for a brief moment. It must have reminded John afterwards of that mountain-top experience when Jesus drew aside the drapery of His humanity and let a little of the inner glory shine out. Here He takes them with Him into the holy of holies of His own inner life with His Father.

Let not any one think that Jesus was simply letting them hear Him pray, so they might learn. Not that; not that. He was taking them into the sacred privacy of His own innermost life. That was a bit of the wooing, under the desperate happenings just ahead. But now as He takes them in He quite forgets them, though He knows they are there. He is absorbed with the Father. He isn't thinking now of the effect of all this on them. That's past. He is alone in spirit with the Father, talking out freely even as though actually quite alone.

We are in the innermost holy of holies here. The heart of the world's life is its literature. The heart of all literature is this sacred Book of God. The heart of this Book is the Gospels. The heart of these four Gospels is John's. The heart of John's is this exquisite bit, chapters thirteen to seventeen. And there's yet an inner heart here. It is this bit, the seventeenth chapter, where the inner side of Jesus' prayer-life lies open to us. And we shall find an innermost heart yet again here.

The simplicity of speech here catches the ear. The holy intimacy of contact with God hushes the spirit. The certainty of the Father's presence awes the heart greatly. The unquestioning confidence in the outcome is to one's faith like a glass of kingdom wine fresh from the King's own hand. The tenseness and yet exquisite quietness holds one's being still with a great stillness. Both shoes and hat go off instinctively and we stand with head bowed low and heart hushed for this is holiest ground.

Of course, no paraphrase of this prayer can possibly approach its own beauty and simplicity. But it may perhaps send one back to the prayer itself to see better what is there.

They're out in the open, down near the Kidron. Jesus stops and looks up towards the blue, the Father's open door, and quietly talks out of His heart into His Father's heart, "Father: the hour is come"; talked of long before this errand was started upon, brooded over these human years, felt in His inner being as it ticked itself nearer in the tremendous passing events. Now it is come. The clock is striking the hour, striking on earth and echoed distinctly in the Father's ear.

"Father: reveal now the true character of the Son; yet only that the Son may reveal Thy true character.[121] Thou hast already done so in the control Thou hast given Him over all men, that so He may give to them the eternal life. And this is the real life to come into intimate touch of heart and life with Thee and with Thine anointed One, Jesus."

"I have already revealed Thy character in doing fully the errand Thou didst send Me on. (And it was fully done in all the active part, though the greatest thing yet remained to be done in the tremendous yielding, the strong passive yielding to Hate's worst that so Love's truest and best might be clearly seen by men.) And now I am coming back to be recognized and acknowledged and received by Thine own self even as it was before I came away on this errand."

Thus far He has been alone with the Father face-to-face; just the two together in closest communion. Now the prayer moves on from communion and petition to intercession. He is thinking of others, of these men who are grouped near by. He has prayed for them before. He is simply picking up the thread of the accustomed prayer He had prayed, and would still pray when He had gone from them up through the doorway of the blue.

He has revealed the Father to them, and they have understood and believed and have followed. Now He prays for them, that they may be kept; not taken out of the world; kept in it, giving their witness to it, yet never of its spirit, always controlled by another Spirit. They were being sent into the world for witness even as He had been.

And a great word breaks out like the bursting of a flood of sunlight out of dark clouds,—joy. He had used it that evening before in the upper room, and again along the road. Now it flashes out again. This reveals the meaning of that good-cheer and overcome with which the roadway talk closed. With the clouds of hate at their blackest, and the storm just about to break in uncontrolled wild fury, He speaks of "My joy." He is singing. In the thick of hatred and plotting here's the bit of music, in the major key, rippling out. Such a spirit cannot be defeated. Joy is faith singing in the storm because it sees already the clearing light beyond.

And so He prays on, touching the same keys of the musical instrument of His heart, back and forth, yet ever advancing in the theme. Now He broadens out, in clear vision, beyond the gathering storm, to those, through all the earth, and down the centuries, who would believe through these men who are listening. What a sweep of faith. That singing cleared His vision.

And then He sees them all, of many races and languages and radical differences, all blended into one body of earnest loving believers drawn by the one vision of Himself back in the glory of the Father's presence, where they will all gather. And then love ties the knot on the end. A personal love ties together Father and Son and—us, who humbly give the glad homage of our hearts.

Right in the very midst of the prayer lies that innermost heart of which I spoke a moment ago. It is in verse ten. Jesus says, "All things that are Mine are Thine, and Thine are Mine." There lies the very inner heart of all carried to the last degree. There is glad giving and full taking; surrender and appropriation. He who gives all may reach in and take all. Here is, humanly, the secret of Jesus' stupendous character and career.

And it is the same for the humblest of us. The road is no different. We may say, by His great grace, in the insistence of our sovereign wills, "All that is mine is Thine: I give it Thee. I give it back to Thee: I use all the strength of my will in yielding all to Thee, and in doing it habitually."

Then we can say, with greatest reverence and humility and yet bold confidence, "All that is Thine is mine." Yet being mine it is Thine. Still being Thine it is mine. So comes the perfection of the rhythmic action of love. Our love gives our all to Him. And then takes the greater all of His—no, not from Him, for Him, held in trust, used for Him, while we keep knees and face close to the ground, lest we stumble and slip and worse.

So the prayer closes. And if we might go back over it, alone in secret, prayerfully, quietly thinking thoughtfully into it, until this great simple prayer gets its hold upon our hearts. And then gradually it would come to us that so He is now praying for us, you and me.

What must it have meant to these men to stand there quietly, awed as they listen to Him praying that prayer. How it reveals the deep consciousness of the intimacy of relation between Father and Son. How it must have touched and stirred them to the very depths to hear Jesus telling the Father so simply about their faith in Himself, and their obedience, their break with their national allegiance to follow Himself. And that word joy—did they wonder about it? And wonder more later that night, and the days after? But the key-note of the music caught, and soon they were singing the same tune, and in the same pitch.

What wooing! This was the closest wooing. The fine wooing of this matchless Lover came to its superlative degree that night. Positive degree, that touch upon their feet; comparative, that talk about the board and along the road; superlative, this taking them in for a brief moment into the secrecy of His inner communion with the Father.

Simplified Spelling.

And this closer wooing is not over. It hasn't quit yet. That vine is still hanging out in fine view, all softly ablaze with the clear beautifying light, not of a fine Passover moon; no, the light of His face, His life, His words. That vine becomes for all time to every heart the pictured meaning of abide. And that word abide gives the whole of the true life.

We say Christian life, and rightly. I like to say also, the true, the natural, life. Any other is abnormal, unnatural, untrue. I might say, "of the higher Christian life," following the common usage of these latter days. I still prefer to say true life. Higher means that there is a lower life. And that this lower is reckoned Christian, too. That is the bother, the cheapening of things; we call a thing Christian which is less than the thing it is called.

Some of us need to go to school, and to sit down in the lower classes where spelling is taught. We can spell believe in the common way with seven letters. We must learn to spell it with four letters—l-o-v-e. We need to learn to spell love with a b and a y—o-b-e-y. We need to learn to spell obey with five letters a-b-i-d-e. We need to find that abide is spelled best with four letters o-b-e-y.

We need to learn this simplified spelling a bit, then all will become simplified, living, loving, witnessing, praying, winning, singing with joy over the results of our new spelling in the syllables of daily life. Blessed Master, we would come to school to Thee to-day. Please let us start down in the spelling class. And teach us, Thou Thyself teach us.

But the vine—let us make that the central picture on the wall, with the Master in the picture pointing to the vine. And under the picture the one word abide. Then the whole story is in easy shape to help, pictured before our eyes. Abide—that is Jesus walking around in your shoes, looking out through your eyes, touching in your hand, speaking through your lips and your presence. He is free to; that's your side of it. He's unhindered. He does it; that's His side of it.

Look up at the picture on the wall. The whole vine is in the fruit, is it not? The whole of the fruit is in the vine, is it not? That's abiding. The whole of Jesus will be in you as you go about your daily common task, singing. The whole of you is in Jesus as everything simple and great, is done to please Him, singing as you do it.

And just as between vine and fruit there are branch and blossom, pruning and careful handling, sun and shade, dew and rain, so there are betweens here before full ripening of fruit comes. There's purifying, cleansing by blood, cleansing by a soft fire burning within, and pruning by the Gardener and by His human assistant, you, sharp, incisive, hurting pruning.

There's feeding,—the juice of the vine flows in, and is taken in; the divine word of the divine Master is meditated, the cud of it is chewed daily. There's obedience,—perfect rhythm of action between vine and branches. There's prayer, the intercourse of our spirits, His and ours, together, the drawing from Him all we need, and the letting Him use us in His interceding for His world. These are some of the betweens. Through these comes the ripening fruit.

And the outer crowd comes eagerly for the fruit hanging over the fence within easy reach. There's a warm sympathy with one's fellows; only the thing's more than the words sound. The Jesus-spirit within will be felt by those outside, something warm and gentle and helpful. There will be things done, many things, earnestly thoughtfully done. The proper word is service. But the thing's so much more than the word ever seems to mean.

And there'll be yet more, a more of a surprising sort. The classical fox called the grapes sour because he couldn't reach them. There'll be some outside sour talk because some of the crowd won't reach the fruit. It wouldn't agree with them the way they insist on living. The Jesus-life abiding within and flowing freely out is a protest against the opposite. The mere presence of a Christ-abiding man convicts people of the sin of their lives and their treatment of Jesus. It convinces them that the absent Jesus is right, and so they are wrong. So there's trouble out in the crowd just because of the ripe good fruit hanging in plain sight and easy reach over the vineyard fence. And that double result goes on getting more so, some coming to the vine drawn by the fruit, some talking against fruit and vine. But the man abiding is of good cheer. He sings. For the outcome is assured.

So every grape-vine, in garden, by roadway, or on hillside, with its vine-stock, branches, blossom, and fruit, tells of the Father's ideal for men, a unity of life with Himself, and with each other. And every bunch of grapes hanging on one stem, with its many in one, tells of that same ideal, the concord of love with the Father and with each other.

And that unity of love dominating all is irresistible to the outer crowd, in the winsomeness of its wooing.

V

The Greatest Wooing

—"The Hound of Heaven

"I will betroth thee unto me forever; yea, I will betroth thee unto me in righteousness, and in justice, and in loving kindness, and in mercies. I will even betroth thee unto me in faithfulness."—Hosea ii. 19, 20.

—Charles Wesley.

V

The Greatest Wooing
(John xviii.-xix.)
Wider Wooing.

At the top of the mountain is the peak. The peak is the range at its highest reach. The peak grows out of the range and rests upon it and upon the earth under all. The whole of the long mountain range and of the earth lies under the peak. The peak tells the story of the whole range. At the last the highest and utmost. All the rest is for this capstone.

The great thing in Jesus' life is His death. The death crowns the life. The whole of the life lies under and comes to its full in the death. The highest point is touched when death is allowed to lay Him lowest. It was the life that died that gives the distinctive meaning to the death. Let us take off hat and shoes as we come to this peak event.

There's a change in John's story here. The evening has gone, the quiet evening of communion. The night has set in, the dark night of hate. The intimacies of love give place to the intrigues of hate. The joy of communion is quickly followed by the jostling of the crowd. Out of the secret place of prayer into the hurly-burly of passion. And the Master's rarely sensitive spirit feels the change. Yet with quiet resolution He steps out to face it. This is part of the hour, part of His great task, the greatest part.

For the holy task of wooing is not changed. It still is wooing, but there's a difference now. There's a shifting. The wooing goes from closer to wider, from the disciples to the outer crowd, from the direct wooing of the national leaders by personal plea to the indirect by action, tremendously personal action.

It moves out into a yet wider sweep. It goes from the wooing of a nation to the wooing of a race, from Jew distinctively to Roman representatively, from Annas standing in God's flood light rejected to Pilate in nature's lesser light obscured, from God's truant messenger nation to the world's mighty ruling nation.

In the epochal event just at hand Jesus begins His great wooing of a race. And that wooing has gone on ever since, wherever He has been able to get through the human channels to the crowd. He was lifted up and at once men began coming a-running broken in heart by the sight. He is being lifted up, and men of all the race are coming as fast as the slow news gets to them.

But back now to John's story. They pick their way over the stones of the little Kidron into the garden of the olives. There, quite alone in the deep shadows of the inner trees, Jesus has His great spirit-conflict, and great victory. The touch with sin so close, so real, now upon Him within a few hours, the sin of others upon His sinless soul,—this shakes Him terrifically beyond our understanding, who don't know purity as He did. But the tremendous strength of yielding brings victory, as ever. And the battle of the morrow is fought in spirit, and won.

Now the trailers of hate come seeking with torch and lantern, soldiers and officers, chief priests and rulers, the ever present rabble, and in the lead the shameless traitor. They are pushing their quest now, seeking Jesus in the hiding whence He had gone days before[122] led by the man who knew His accustomed haunts.

But there's no need for seeking now. Jesus is full ready. He decides the action that follows. He is masterful even in His purposeful yielding. Quietly He walks out from the cover of the trees to meet them. And as their torches turn full upon His advancing figure again that marvellous power not only of restraint but decidedly more is felt by them. And the whole company, traitor, soldiers, rulers, rabble, overpowered in spirit, fall back and then drop to the ground utterly overawed and cowed by the lone man they are seeking.

Does Judas expect this? Will this power they are unable to resist not open the eyes of these rulers! But there's no stupidity equal to that which goes with stubbornness. In a moment Jesus reveals His purpose in this, to shield His disciples. Now the power of restraint is withdrawn and He yields to their desires. They shall have fullest sway in using their freedom of action as they will. And Peter's foolish attempts are quietly overruled.

They keep up the forms by taking Jesus to Annas the real Jewish ruler of the nation. But it is simply an opportunity for the coarseness of their hate to vent itself upon His person. They pretend an examination here in the night's darkness suited to their deeds. He quietly reminds them of the frank openness of all His teachings.

Meanwhile John's friendly act has gotten Peter entrance. The attitude of the two men is in sharpest contrast. John is avowedly Jesus' friend, regardless of personal danger. Peter just the reverse. And the hate of the leaders has soaked into all their surroundings even down to the housemaids. And John notes how exactly Jesus foreknew all, even to a thrice-spoken denial before the second crowing of a cock.

Now comes the great Pilate phase. It was the intense malignity of their hate that made them bother with Pilate. They could easily have killed Jesus and Pilate would never have concerned himself about it. But they couldn't have put Him to such exquisite suffering and such shameful indignity before the crowds as by the Roman form of death by crucifixion.

Clearly there is a hate at work behind theirs. Their hate is distinctly inhuman. Is all hate? There's an unseen personal power in action here set on spilling out the utmost that malignant hate can upon the person of Jesus. But these men are cheerful tools. Hate is tying its hardest knot with ugliest black thread on the end of its opportunity.

This is Pilate's opportunity and he seems to sense it. And a struggle begins between conscience and cowardice, between right action with an ugly fight for it, and yielding to wrong with an easy time of it. Clearly he feels the purity and the personal power of this unusual prisoner. The motive of envy and hate under their action is as plain to his trained eyes.

Twice the two men, Pilate and Jesus, are alone together. Did ever man have such an opportunity, personally, and historically? With rare touch and winsomeness Jesus woos. And Pilate feels it to the marrow under all his rough speech. His repeated attempts with the leaders make that clear. But cowardice gripped him hard. It's a way cowardice has.

The name of Caesar conjures up fears,—loss of position, of wealth, of reputation, maybe of life itself. He surrenders. Conscience is slain on the judgment seat. Cowardice laughs and wins. A sharp fling brings a cry of allegiance to Caesar from their reluctant throats, as their hatred wins the day. He strikes them back an ugly blow as He surrenders. That reluctant Caesar cry told out the intensity of their hate. They hated Caesar much, but they hated Jesus immeasurably more. They gulp down Caesar to be able to vent their spleen upon Jesus.

And so they crucified Him. At last they succeed. They have gotten what they were bent on. The hate burning within, these months and years, finds its full vent. Its hateful worst is done, and horribly well done. And they stand about the cross with unconcealed gloating in pose and face and speech and eyes. Their part of the story is done.

Masterful Dying.

But Jesus' part—ah! that was just begun. John lays emphasis on the mastery of Jesus here. It is marked, and reveals to John's faithful love-opened eyes the dominating purpose of Jesus in yielding to death. Strong, thoughtful, self-controlled, anticipating every move, He was using all the strength of His great strong will in yielding. He was doing it masterfully, intelligently.

This is marked throughout. At the arrest He walks frankly out to meet those seeking Him, and restrains them in that strangely powerful way till He was quite ready. He makes the personal plea to Pilate for Pilate's sake, impressing him so greatly, but interposing nothing to change the purpose of His accusers. When Pilate's final decision is given John notes that Jesus "went out bearing the cross for Himself," though provision had been made for this.[123] His influence upon Pilate is seen in the accuracy of the kingly inscription that hangs over the cross. In the midst of the excruciating bodily pain He thinks of His mother, and with marvellous self-control speaks the quiet word to her and to John that insures her future under his filial care.

And then John significantly adds, "Jesus, knowing that all things are now finished."[124] With masterly forethought, and self-control and deliberation He had done the thing He had set Himself to do. Never was yielding so masterful. Never was a great plan carried out so fully through the set purpose of one's enemies. His every action bears out the word He had spoken, "No man taketh My life away from Me, I lay it down of Myself."[125]

So now His great work is done, and thoroughly done. His lips speak the tremendous word, "It is finished." And He bowed His head and gave up His spirit. It was His own act. The self-restraint was strong upon Him till all was done that was needed for the great purpose in hand. Then His head is bowed, His great heart broke under the terrific strain on His spirit as He allowed His life to go out.

From that moment no indignity touches His body. The Jews with their wearisome insistence on empty technicalities would have added further indignity to crucifixion. But that body is sacredly guarded from their profane hand by unseen restraint. John with solemn simplicity points to the unmistakable physical evidence, in the separation of blood and water, that Jesus had actually died; no swooning, but death. And reverently he finds the confirmation of Scripture.

Only tender love touches that body now. Two gentlemen of highest official and social standing and of large wealth, brothers in their faith in Jesus, and also in their timidity, now take steps at once to have the precious body of their dear friend tenderly cared for without regard to expense. So He is laid away in a new tomb in a garden among the flowers of the spring time. The last touch is one of tender love. So His greatest wooing was done, and begun; the great act done, its tremendous wooing influence only just begun.

Jesus died deliberately. This is quite clear. It was done of love aforethought. It was His own act fitted into the circumstances surrounding Him. This makes His death mean just what He meant it to mean. Run back through His teachings rather carefully and that meaning stands clearly out.

He was the Father's messenger; simply this; but all of this. The ideals of right so insistently and incessantly held up and pressed were the Father's ideals. His mere presence told the Father's great love for men. They two were so knit that when the one suffered the other suffered, too.

It was the love for men in His own heart that drew Him down here and drove Him along even to the Calvary Hill. He died for men, in their place, on their behalf. This was His one thought. Through this their bondage to sin and to Satan would be broken and they would be set free.[126] And they would be drawn, their hearts would be utterly melted and broken by His love for them.[127] The influence would reach out until all the race would feel its power and respond; and it would reach into each one's life who came till the life he lived was of the abundant, eternal sort.

The devil was a real personality to Jesus. This whole terrific struggle ending at the cross was a direct spirit-battle with that great spirit prince. So Jesus understood it. All the bitter enmity to Himself traces straight back to that source. That enmity found its worst expression in Jesus' death. The pitched spirit-battle was there. But that prince was judged, condemned, utterly defeated and cast out in that battle, and his hold upon men broken.[128]

And so this was the greatest wooing of all. It was greatest in its intensity of meaning to the Father looking eagerly down. It revealed His unbending, unflinching ideals of right, and the great strength and tenderness of His love for men. He would even give His Son. It was greatest in its intensity of meaning to the Son. It meant the utmost of suffering ever endured, the utmost of love underneath ever revealed; and it would mean the race-wide sweep of His gracious power.

It was greatest in its intensity of meaning to Satan, the hater of God and man. It told his utter defeat, and loss of power over man. So it broke our bonds and made us free to yield to the wooing. And it was greatest in its intensity of meaning to us men. For it showed to our confused eyes the one ideal of right standing out clear and full. It set us free from the fetters of our bondage, gave us the tremendous incentive of love to reach up to the ideal of right, and more, immensely more, gave us power to reach it.

It was the greatest wooing in the out-reach of its influence, for all men of all the earth would be touched.[129] And it was greatest in the in-reach to all the life of each one who came under its blessed influence. The whole ministry taught this. It would mean newness of life in body, in mind, in social nature, in spirit, and in the eternal quality of life lived here, and to be lived without any ending.

And all the world has responded to this greatest wooing as they have come to know of it. That three-languaged inscription on the cross was a world appeal and a world prophecy. In Hebrew the religious language of the world whose literature told of the one true God, in Latin the language of the masters of the world, in Greek the language of the culture of the world, that message went out to all the world. This Jesus is our Kinsman-King, our Brother-Ruler, our Love-

Autocrat. He revealed His love for us in His death for us.

And men answer to Jesus' great plea. With flooded eyes and broken hearts, and bending wills, and changed lives, men of all the race bow gratefully at the feet of Jesus, our Saviour and Lord and coming King.

VI

An Appointed Tryst Unexpectedly Kept
A Day of Startling Joyous Surprises
—"The Hound of Heaven.
"After I am raised up I will go before you into Galilee."—Mark xiv. 28.

VI

An Appointed Tryst Unexpectedly Kept
(John xx.)
The Appointment.

Jesus had made an appointment. It was with these dear friends who had responded so lovingly to His wooing. It was a significant appointment, most significant. He had appointed to meet them three days after His death. He had made a further appointment to meet them in Galilee. What a stupendous appointment to make!

It was a sacred appointment, sacred as the love that made it, sacred to Jesus as the friendship of these men with whom it was made, sacred as His word that never was broken. Our Scottish friends use a most significant word for appointment, the word tryst. They used to use it some for ordinary appointments, but chiefly it is used for friendship and for love-appointments. The appointment is a tryst.

Tryst is the same word as trust. In the old Gothic language it was one of the words used for a covenant or treaty. In medieval Latin it was a pledge given that an agreement would be kept. It is a fine turn of a word that uses the very spirit of confidence in one's heart in another as the name for the appointment made with him. The trust in the heart gives the name to the appointment. It's an appointment with one who can be trusted to keep his word, and who is trusted.

So an appointed tryst becomes more than a mere appointment. It is a pledge of faith. Now this is the real force of the word here. Jesus had appointed a tryst with these men, and in making it He was plighting His troth, pledging His word to them. He had asked them to risk all for Him. In this tryst He is pledging all to them.

He never forgot that sacred appointment. He had thought much before He made it. He knew it would involve much to keep it. The power of God was at stake in the making and the keeping of it. He knew that. He thought of it. He made the appointment and He kept it. Jesus keeps His appointments. His word never fails. Not even the gates of death, nor the power of the evil one, can prevail against it.

This was a staggering appointment. It took so much for granted. It reckons God's power is as big as it is. But then that's a way Jesus had, and has. And it is a way he will come to have who companions much with Jesus.

Jesus had spoken of this indirectly but distinctly when first He told His disciples of His suffering and death, six months before. And each time afterwards when He told them of His death the words were always added, "and the third day rise again."[130] I The two things are nearly always linked. But they hadn't seemed to sense what He meant. The thing seems quite beyond them.

He spoke of it again on that never-to-be-forgotten night of the betrayal, the night of the feet-washing, and that last long talk, and that wondrous Kidron-prayer. He spoke of it more than once that night.

It was a very emphatic word He spoke as they were walking along the darkly shadowed

Jerusalem streets out towards the east gate. He said, "a little while and ye shall behold Me no more; and again a little while and ye shall see Me."[131] And the disciples pick this up and puzzle over it.

And the Master explains rather carefully and at some length. There was a time of sore trouble coming for Him and for them. And while they were sorrowing the outer crowd would be making merry. But it would be just as with the expectant mother, He said. All the while even when the pains cut she is thinking of the great delight that is to be hers. Her after-joy clean wipes out of her thought the sharp cutting of the pain.

So it would be. "I will see you again," He said in plainest speech. And again that same night He said, "after I am raised up, I will go before you into Galilee." Could any appointment be more explicit as to time and place?

But they forget. Aye, there's the bother, this thing of forgetting. The memory is ever the index of the heart and the will and the understanding. You can tell the one by the other. Some things are never forgot. A bit embarrassing and odd this thing of forgetting what Jesus says.

His enemies remembered, and took special pains to head off any breaking of their careful plans.[132] And even when the angels remind the women of the promised appointment, and they with great joy repeat the reminder to the disciples, it seems like "idle talk" and is not accepted. The thing couldn't be, they think.[133] Finally the evidence becomes so convincing that they start off for the trysting place, "into Galilee, unto the mountain where Jesus had appointed them."[134]

How the Appointment Was Kept.

Let us look a bit at the wonderful keeping, so unexpected, of this sacred tryst. It's the third day now since Jesus' death. It is in the dark dusk of the early morning. A little knot of women make their way slowly along the road leading out of the city gate. Mary Magdalene is in the lead, so far ahead of the others as to be alone. They are carrying packages of perfumed ointments. They are thinking only of a dear dead body and of clinging fragrant memories.

They are troubling themselves about how to get the big stone at the tomb pushed aside. It was too much for their strength. As she drew near the tomb Mary Magdalene's love-quickened eyes notice something quite unexpected. The stone is moved aside! She naturally thinks some one has taken the body secretly away in the night.

Quickly she turns and runs back towards the city to tell Peter and John. And as quickly as they hear the startling news they are off on a smart run towards the tomb. Meanwhile the other women go on into the tomb. They are further startled to see a glorious looking person who assures them that Jesus is living, having risen up out of death. All a-quiver with fear intermingled with the first glimmering light of a great hope that they hardly dare hope, they flee hastily back to town to tell the others.

Now Peter and John, who have been eagerly running, arrive breathless, with John in the lead. Gazing reverently, intently, in through the opening John sees, not a body, but on the spot where the body had been laid, the linen wrappings lying, held up in the shape of a body by Nicodemus' abundant and heavy ointments just as when they held the body of Jesus. But clearly there is nothing in them now.

Now Peter comes up, and, just like him, goes straight in, and is at once struck by the arrangement of these cloths, just as John had been. Then they comment on the fact that the head cloths are lying where they naturally would be, a little apart from the others, the distance of the head from the body.

The evidence convinces them that Jesus' spirit had indeed returned to His body, and that He had risen up through the cloths, and gone. And they start back to town in a great maze of wonder and delight.

And now Mary Magdalene, knowing nothing of all this, comes slowly back absorbed with her thoughts that the body has been secretly removed. She stands at the open tomb weeping. Then for the first time she stoops down and looks in. She is startled to see two angels left there to explain matters.

They gently say "Why weepest thou?" Still sobbing, she says, "They have taken away my Lord, and I know not where they have laid Him." And turning aside as she speaks she sees some One standing near her. Her tear-misted eyes think Him the attendant in charge of the garden. Again the question by this man, "Why weepest thou?" How strangely they talk, these angels and this gardener! She makes a plea for the body.

Then the one word, her name, spoken in that voice she knew so well—"Mary." Ah! there's no question about that voice. She needs no explanation nor evidence more than this, as she cries out, "Oh, my beloved Master." Then He acts so like Himself; He gives her an errand to do for Him. And off she goes. She has had the wondrous privilege of the first sight of Him, and the first errand for Him. The tryst has been kept with Mary Magdalene.

And now the other women who had gone running down the road after hearing the angels' startling message are amazed to meet Jesus standing in the roadway in front of them. And the same quiet rich voice so gently and simply gives them the usual "good-morning" salutation. At once they are on their knees at His feet. And He softly says, "Don't be afraid. Go tell My brethren to meet Me at the old place appointed, up by the blue waters of Galilee." And again the tryst is kept.

But before all this, the soldiers on guard, terror-stricken by the earthquake that had taken place, and dazed at the sight of the "angel of the Lord" had fled at top speed to the chief priests with their startling story. Here was a wholly unexpected bothersome finish to the thing. But quick consultation follows. And then free use of money makes the soldiers willing to tell what they know to be a lie. And so the two utterly different stories, the truth and the lie, get into circulation at once. The soldiers and the chief priests' circle have learned that the appointment was kept.

Meanwhile Peter has gone down the road back to town in a maze of conflicting emotions. John, lighter of foot, had hurried ahead, very likely to tell the great news to Jesus' mother, now his own. Peter plods slowly along, thinking hard. It was still early morning, the air so still and fragrant with the dew. Maybe down by some big trees he is walking, absorbed, when all at once, some One is by his side. It's the Master. The appointment has been kept with Peter. But we must leave them alone together. Peter has some things to straighten out. That's a sacred interview meant only for him.

That afternoon two disciples walking out to a little village a few miles away are joined by a Stranger whose talk makes their hearts burn like the Master's used to. And as they gather about the evening meal with Him, and He gives thanks and breaks the loaf, all at once their eyes see. It is Jesus Himself who has been with them all the time. Again the appointment is kept.

At once they hasten back to town, and are just telling the news in joyously broken speech to the disciples gathered in an upper room with locked doors when again, all at once, Jesus appears in their midst, and eats some bread and fish, and tells them to know by the feel that it is really Himself with them. He has kept His sacred appointment with the Twelve. Then a week later He comes in like manner among them again for the sake of one man, Thomas. So He keeps the appointment with Thomas, also.

Our Guarantee of His Promises.

Two things stand out sharply. The resurrection was not expected. It was the most tremendous surprise. The news was received at first by those most interested with utter stubborn unbelief. Then the evidence was so clear and repeated, and incontestable that these same men staked their lives on it. They suffered to the extreme for their witness that Jesus had indeed risen.

Jesus rose from the dead. His body was re-inhabited by His spirit. The spirit didn't die. Spirits neither sleep nor die. The body died. Then life came into it again. It was a real body that could eat and be touched. It was recognized as the same one they had known. But it was changed. The old limitations were gone. New powers had come.

Jesus keeps His appointments. His pledged word never fails. Not a word He has spoken can ever be broken. Some day He is coming back. It is an appointment.[135] Then we, too, who have slipped the tether of life and left our bodies temporarily in the dust, shall rise up again to meet Him. It is a sacred appointment He has made with us.

And some of us who live in that day shall be changed instead of dying, and shall be caught up to meet Him and our own loved ones in the air. That's His true tryst with us up in the blue, some day. And He will keep it.

And meanwhile everything He has promised us in the Book is sure, as being His plighted word. His resurrection is our bond, our guarantee. As surely as He rose on that third morning He will keep His word regarding every matter to you and me.

His appointments never fail, whether of guidance, of bodily health and strength, of supplies for every sort of need, of peace, of power, of victory. The power that raised Jesus up from out the dead is pledged to us for every promise of this Book for to-day's life. He will do an act of creation before He will let His Word fail. He will leave no power unused to keep the appointment of His Word with us.

Let us trust His Word to us fully. And let us live our trust.

VII

Another Tryst

A Story of Fishing, of Guests at Breakfast, and of a Walk and Talk by the Edge of Blue Galilee

"I come unto you."—John xiv. 18.

"Lo, I am with you all the days."—Matthew xxviii. 20.

VII

Another Tryst
(John xxi.)
Jesus Unrecognised.

John's story is done. And it is well done. With the skill of a tried jurist he has drawn up a clear full line of evidence and presented it in a vigorous straightforward way. And he plainly states his case. His whole purpose is that those who read his little book shall come into warm personal touch of life with the Lord Jesus. That ties the knot on tight at the end of chapter twenty. John's case has gone to the jury of his readers.

But now John reaches for his pen again. The guiding Spirit has put another bit into his heart to write down. This time it is a special bit, not for all to whom the book is sent, but for a selected class of his readers, namely, for those of them who have given John a favourable verdict on the evidence presented. It grows out of chapter xx. 31 as rose out of bud, and fruit out of blossom. It is for those who "believe that Jesus is the Christ the Son of God," and so "have life in His Name."

And a very tender precious bit it is, more wondrous in its sheer simplicity than any of us seem to suspect. It is simply this: this Jesus is with us all the time. This same Jesus who was so swayed by the need of the crowd, who burned His life out day by day warmly responding to their sore need—He is here.

This Jesus who fed the hungry, healed the sick of every sort, and freed men from devilish power, who convicted men so tremendously of their wrong, restrained their evil power to hurt, wooed the hearts of all so irresistibly, and led them into changed lives; this Jesus who died and then did the stupendously mighty thing of rising up out of death,—this Jesus is with us now by your side and mine.

And He is just the same Jesus in His warm love and resistless power. The words are rather familiar. The fact—no one of us seems to have gotten hold of it yet. This is the thing that makes John eagerly reach for his pen again before his little book-messenger goes out on its errand.

The thing isn't new in information, but in actual living experience it seems to be so new as to be an unknown thing to some of us. The Master had spoken of this that betrayal-night around the supper board. It was really a continuation of that trysting appointment He had made with them that evening, a wonderful continuation.

Clearly they didn't understand Him that night. But during those after-Pentecost days they were given a continuous graphic unforgetable illustration of its meaning. We to-day seem able to explain the part they didn't understand, the teaching that betrayal-night. We don't seem to get hold of the part they did understand and experience, the real presence of the risen Jesus in the midst actively at work.

That night Jesus said: "I will make request of the Father, and He will send you another unfailing powerful Friend to be always at your side." Then He added: "He abides with you now (in My presence) and shall be in you (after I send Him)." Then He said, "I come unto you. Yet a little while and the world seeth Me no more but ye see Me."

And again, "He that hath My commandments and keepeth them he it is that (in that sheweth that he) loveth Me and ... I will manifest or shew Myself unto him." Here is the simple teaching: He would send the Holy Spirit; in the Holy Spirit's coming Jesus Himself, the new risen exalted empowered enthroned Jesus, He came; and He would let them see Himself with them.

Now this added chapter of John's is the illustration in advance to these men of what these words mean. The great standing illustration is that Book of Acts which, will you notice, doesn't end. It only breaks off, abruptly, without even a punctuation point. It wasn't meant to end. We are supposed to be living in it yet. But these men haven't come to the experience of the Pentecostal Acts yet. This is an illustration in advance to them. And it remains an illustration to us of what we seem a bit slow in taking in.

But let us get at the simple bit of story itself. There's a little group of the inner circle, seven including the leaders. These men haven't found their feet yet. The stupendous events of those days, coming in such startling succession, have left them dazed. The crucifixion left them stupidly dazed; the resurrection left them joyous, but still dazed. They don't know just where they are, nor what to do.

So Peter proposes fishing; an ideal proposition, when you want to get off and think things through and out. Any fisherman knows that. And the others readily join in. They see the good sense of it. But the fish don't catch. And the morning finds them tired in body and more tired in the spiritless uncertainty that hangs over them like a clinging damp fog.

Yonder is some One standing on the beach. But that's nothing unusual. They barely notice Him. And now this Stranger calls out to them a cheery common question, "Caught anything?" And now He gives a—no, it can hardly be called a command, so quietly is it said. Yet they are subtly conscious of a something in the word that makes them obey, though it's the last sort of thing to do.

And now at once the net-ropes pull so hard; astonishing this! Then John's keen spirit detects Who it is. Is he thinking of the other big unexpected haul in those same waters![136] And Peter's over the side of the boat shoreward. Fishing has lost all attraction for him.

And when they all got ashore with their haul, tired, wet, chilled to the marrow, hungry, what's this? A blazing fire of coals burning cheerfully on the sands. And some fish dexterously poised, doing to a brown turn, and some bread. And the Stranger, no, Jesus, He's no longer a stranger, Jesus says quietly, "Boys, better bring the haul up on the beach."

And the old fishing habit still strong on them counts the fish. It's such an unusual haul, they must know how many. John must be thinking again about that earlier haul. The net couldn't stand the strain then. But now it's different. Ah! _every_ thing's blessedly different now. "The net was not rent."

Then the gracious call to breakfast by their Host. Was ever fish done to such a fine turn? Did ever any fish have such an exquisite flavour? or taste so good? Did ever men eat so gladly and yet quietly with a distinct touch of awe in their spirits? For they know it is the Master, though no word of that has been spoken. Words were needless.

Now they're walking along the beach, Jesus and Peter in the lead but the others quite near. And there's the bit of talk between the two. Very gently Jesus says, "Do you love Me, Peter?" And Peter feels he hardly dare use the sacred word for "love" that the Master has used. He had made such an awful break at just that point. And with breaking voice he says, "Yea, Lord, Thou knowest I have the highest regard for Thee."

And again the question, and the answer, with Peter still humbly clinging to his more modest word. And now Jesus says, "Do you really love Me even as you yourself say?" And Peter with his heart in his face says passionately, "Lord, Thou knowest better than I can tell Thee."

And because he loves, Peter is given the full privilege of shepherding the whole flock, from feeding little lambkins on to feeding all, and guiding, through the hard places, even the wayward ones. And more yet and higher, because Peter loves, he will be privileged to suffer, even as his Master had suffered. The fellowship would extend even to that.

And Peter's eye falls on John. And apparently he is thinking of the contrast between John's faithfulness and his own break that betrayal-night. If poor faulty Peter may be so privileged how John would be rewarded. But Jesus quietly turns Peter, and all Peter's numerous kinsfolk of this sort, away from human comparisons. And instead He seeks to turn their hearts to this: He is coming back in person some day for an advance step in the kingdom program. And there they are, walking and talking, along the beach by the blue Galilean waters.

The Same Jesus Here Now.

An unrecognized Stranger who turns out to be Jesus; an unusual haul of fish gotten in a very unusual way; a warm fire and tasty breakfast for cold hungry men; a tender talk about love and service and sacrifice, and about Jesus' return;—all this is a moving-picture illustration of the meaning of a word, one word.

It is a word Jesus used in that last long quiet talk. It's the key-word to this added chapter, occurring three times. In the old version it is the word "shew"; in the revision "manifest." "After these things Jesus manifested Himself again ... and He manifested Himself on this wise." "This is now the third time that Jesus was manifested to the disciples after that He was risen from the dead."[137]

The word used underneath literally means "to make manifest or visible or know, what has been hidden or unknown."[138] Then each time it is used it gets its local colouring from its connection. The simple tremendous meaning here clearly is this: Jesus let Himself be seen and known. He did not come. He was there.

But their eyes couldn't see Him. In effect He was hidden, not seeable. Now the change that comes is this: He is seen. And He is seen in His true native character; so certain results follow. He had said, "I will manifest Myself."[139] And this was now the third time that He did it, to the disciples, after that He was risen.

This is the advance illustration of the Book of Acts. This is the tremendous thing He is burning into their hearts through eyes and ears:—He is always present. He, whose power they had felt so stupendously, and whose warm sympathy so tenderly, He is always with them. The coming of the Holy Spirit meant just this. The Spirit would be as Jesus' other self, as Jesus Himself. The one thing the Spirit would do would be to manifest, to shew openly, the power of Jesus.

Then four pictures pass before their eyes to illustrate the meaning, a fishing picture and a breakfast picture in action; then in words, a love-service-suffering picture, and a picture of Jesus returning in person seen by all to take an advance-step.

The fishing picture clearly meant this: great numbers of people, surprisingly great numbers, coming, drawn not by any human skill, but by the supernatural power of Jesus manifesting Himself in that way. The breakfast picture meant this: that this wondrous Jesus would take tender personal care of those in this blessed gathering ministry, even to their bodily needs and strength.

And the love-service-suffering word-picture said so plainly this: true service grows out of love. The chief thing is the loyal tender attachment to the person of Jesus. Then out of this will naturally come service, and willingness to suffer. The touchstone won't be service but personal love. The service will simply be an expression of the love.

And the Jesus-return word-picture fills their vision with this same Jesus coming in open glory before all eyes to carry out the kingdom plan. As these men learned to live always in the presence of a Jesus whom their outer eyes saw not, these pictures would become living pictures seen in open daily life.

So this is a further bit of the tryst appointment. This is the fuller tryst, the greater, the yet more wondrous tryst. Not only would He rise up out of death, and appear to them in person seen by the outer eyes, but He would be with them continually manifesting Himself in rarest power of action, in tenderest personal care, in talking and walking with them.

They would see the power plainly at work; then they would say with a soft hush, "He is here." They would find new bodily strength, new guidance in perplexity, new peace in the midst of confusion, and they would say to each other in awed tones, "He is here: it's the Master's touch."

And so it would come to be a habit to anticipate His presence. They would figure Him in, and figure Him in big, as big as He is, in all sorts of circumstances and planning and meeting of difficulties.

It is most striking that John closes his Gospel so differently from the others. They close with the Master rising up and disappearing on a cloud into the upper blue. John closes with Jesus walking along the beach, talking with the little group of trusted ones. Jesus did ascend up into the blue whence He shall some day descend. But the Holy Spirit sends John back to his pen to give us this as the last picture, impressed on the sensitive plate of the eyes of our heart. This: Jesus present with us all the while walking along the shore of our common round of life, clothed with matchless power, and devoting Himself to us as we to Him.

Along about the middle of the eighteenth century there came to England a young French-Swiss, named De la Fléchère, hungry hearted for the truth. He was so helped by John Wesley that he cast in his lot with the new Methodist movement and John Williams Fletcher became one of Wesley's most faithful co-labourers. Late in life he married a woman of unusual mental and spiritual attainment.

I ran across a simple story over there of this Mrs. John Fletcher which interested and helped me much. This saintly gifted woman told of a dream which came to her with such vividness as to seem to her mature mind more than a common passing vagary of sleep. In her dream she was engaged in an intense struggle with an evil spirit. She was having a most difficult fight.

She noticed some one standing a little bit to one side watching the fight but taking no active part in it. The fighting became so intense and her strength so sorely strained that she was on the point of giving up. Then this one came over near and touched her gently and said, "Be strong." Instantly a wondrous strength came to her and she held on.

Again the evil one attacked her viciously. She wondered why this helping friend did not come to her assistance in the fight. Then she was moved to say to her enemy, "Depart, in Jesus' Name." And instantly he fled. And she was free and victorious. That was her dream. As she awoke there came to her the most real sense of the presence of her Lord.

This is only one simple illustration from life. I have run across many of the same, wholly different each from the other, but each emphasizing the one simple tremendous fact of the constant presence with us of this same mighty Jesus.

It is of keenest help to mark that humanly the initiative of action is in our hands. The fight is ours. We decide our stand. We choose, and we bear the brunt or result of our choice. We step out as the need comes. Prayer and a spirit of humblest dependence on Another guides our decision and action. But we take the action. The initiative is ours.

And always alongside is One standing close up, putting all His limitless power at our disposal, in our action. All He did in living and dying and rising up out of death was done on our behalf. And now all the tremendous result of His victory is at our command. All the power native in Him is for our use.

This is the other tryst our Lover-Lord makes with us. "Lo! I am with you all the days, sunny days and shadowy, bright days and dark, all the days clear to the end." This is the sacred tryst He has made with us.

And He keeps the tryst. We may count on Him, And as we do we shall cast nets into hopeless waters and get a great haul. We shall find His presence anticipating all our personal needs. We shall rejoice to serve and—if so it prove to be—to suffer for the One we love with tenderest devotion.

And we shall look eagerly forward to seeing Him who is always in touch with us, here and now, to seeing Him with these outer eyes of ours, coming in glory with His resistless power, to make some blessed changes.

Footnotes

[1] John i. 35-42.
[2] i. 1-18.
[3] i. 19-xii. 50.
[4] Chapters xiii.-xvii.
[5] Chapters xviii.-xix.
[6] Chapters xx.-xxi.
[7] Colossians i. 15-17.
[8] Philippians ii. 6-8.

[9] Ephesians i.19-23.
[10] Revelation i. 13-18.
[11] i. 1-18.
[12] i. 19-xii. 50.
[13] Chapters xiii.-xvii.
[14] Chapters xviii.-xix.
[15] Chapter xx.
[16] Chapter xxi.
[17] There are nineteen of these incidents:
1. The official deputation, i. 19-51. 2. Marriage in Cana, ii. 1-11. 3. Cleansing the Temple, ii. 13-22. 4. Nicodemus, iii. 1-21. 5. Dispute about purifying, iii. 22-36. 6. Samaritan woman, iv. 1-42. 7. Nobleman's son, iv. 46-54. 8. Thirty-eight years infirmity, v. 9. Feeding five thousand, vi. 1-15. 10. Walking on water and discussion, vi. 16-71. 11. At Feast of Tabernacles, vii. 12. Accused woman, viii. 1—11. 13. First attempt to stone, viii. 12-59. 14. Man born blind, ix. 1-x. 21. 15. Second stoning, x. 22-42. 16. Lazarus, xi. 17. Bethany Feast, xii. 1-11. 18. Triumphal Entry, xii. 12-19. 19. The Greeks, xii. 20-50.
[18] iii. 32.
[19] iii. 11.
[20] i. 19-51.
[21] ii.1-11.
[22] ii. 12.
[23] ii. 13-22.
[24] vii. 50, 51; xix. 39.
[25] ii. 23-iii. 21.
[26] iii. 11, 19, 32.
[27] iii. 22-36.
[28] iv 1-42.
[29] iv. 43-45.
[30] iv. 46-54.
[31] v. 1-47.
[32] vi. 1-14.
[33] vi. 15-71.
[34] vii. 1-52.
[35] viii. 1-11.
[36] viii 12-59.
[37] ix. l-x. 21.
[38] x. 22-39.
[39] x. 40-42.
[40] xi. 1-53.
[41] xi. 54-57.

[42] xii. 1-8.
[43] xii. 9-11.
[44] xii. 12-19.
[45] xii. 20-36.
[46] xii. 37-50.
[47] ii. 23.
[48] iv. 45.
[49] vi. 1-2, 14, 15, 34.
[50] vii. 31, 40, 41.
[51] viii. 30.
[52] x. 20, 21.
[53] x. 40-42.
[54] xi. 45; xii. 9-12.
[55] xii 17-18.
[56] xii. 12-14.
[57] xii. 42.
[58] ii. 23-25
[59] vi. 60-66.
[60] xii. 42-43.
[61] i. 35-51; ii. 1-11; iii. 13-28.
[62] vi. 66-69.
[63] xi. 16.
[64] ii. 22; xii. 16.
[65] iii. 1-21.
[66] vii. 50-51 with xii. 42, 43.
[67] xix. 39.
[68] iv. 5-42.
[69] Genesis XV. 6 with xx. 11.
[70] vii. 35.
[71] xii. 24-36.
[72] Note the official deputation incident (chapter i.), and the Nicodemus incident (chapter iii.).
[73] i. 19-34.
[74] iii. 11, 32.
[75] ii. 13-20.
[76] iii. 22-iv. 3.
[77] iv. 44.
[78] v. 16-18.
[79] vi. 30-36, 41-42, 52, 60-66.
[80] vii. throughout.
[81] viii. 1-11.

[82] viii. 12-59.
[83] ix. 1-x. 21.
[84] x. 22-39.
[85] xi. 47-57.
[86] "Jesus had not yet come," intimating that they were expecting Him in accordance with an understanding between Him and them. vi. 17.
[87] Kings vi. 1-7.
[88] Kings xvii. 17-24.
[89] Kings xiii. 20-21.
[90] Kings iv. 32-37.
[91] Luke viii. 40-42, 49-56.
[92] Luke vii. 11-17.
[93] iii. 1-21.
[94] iv. 7-42.
[95] viii. 1-11.
[96] ii. 13-21.
[97] vii. throughout.
[98] Luke iv. 30; John viii. 59; x. 39; xii. 36.
[99] Mark x. 32; Luke ix. 53.
[100] viii. 12-59.
[101] x. 22-39.
[102] xii. 12-19, 36.
[103] xiii. 1-3.
[104] ii. 4; vii. 6, 8, 30; viii. 20.
[105] xii 23, 27; xiii. 1, 31-32; xvii. 1.
[106] xiii. 4-11.
[107] xiii. 12-20.
[108] Philippians ii. 6-11.
[109] xiii. 18.
[110] xiii. 21-30.
[111] The word "glory" with its companion "glorify," is frequent in John. We shall understand better if we remember that originally the word he uses means the opinion that one has of another, especially a good opinion. But as the word is used commonly here the underlying thought is, not what one thinks of another, nor yet something that one may give to another, but the actual character in the one so thought of. Glory is the character of goodness. So to see one's glory is to see his real inner character, and to see that character openly recognized and acknowledged. So to glorify means to recognize and acknowledge openly the true character of one. Twice in John the word is used in the cheaper meaning of outer honour among men. vii. 18; viii. 50.
[112] xiii. 31-33.
[113] xiii. 34-38.